core
practices
in teacher
education

a global
perspective

edited by

PAM GROSSMAN and
URBAN FRAEFEL

Harvard Education Press
Cambridge, Massachusetts

Core Practices in Education

Series edited by Pam Grossman

OTHER BOOKS IN THIS SERIES

Core Practices for Project-Based Larning
A Guide for
Teachers and Leaders
Pam Grossman
Zachary Herrmann
Sarah Schneider Kavanagh
Christopher G. Pupik Dean

Preparing Science Teachers
Through Practice-Based Teacher Education
Edited by David Stroupe,
Karen Hammerness, and Scott McDonald

Teaching Core Practices
in Teacher Education
Edited by Pam Grossman

Paperback ISBN 9781682538685

Library of Congress Cataloging-in-Publication Data is on file.

Published by Harvard Education Press,
an imprint of the Harvard Education Publishing Group

Harvard Education Press
8 Story Street
Cambridge, MA 02138

Cover Design: Wilcox Design
Cover Image: Makrushka&zygotehasnobrain/iStock.com

The typefaces in this book are ITC Stone and Museo.

CONTENTS

Introduction

A Cross-National Perspective
on Teaching Core Practices

Pam Grossman and Urban Fraefel

I n response to persistent critiques that teachers are not well enough prepared for the challenges of the classroom, teacher educators worldwide
have been redesigning their programs over the past decade to focus more
centrally on practice.[1] Such efforts have included both changing and
lengthening field experiences in schools as part of the curriculum and also
bringing more opportunities to study and engage in practice into university-
based classes. The turn toward practice-based teacher education has been
well documented in the United States.[2] What has been less well documented are the global efforts to create more practice-based teacher education programs. From Chile and Australia to the Netherlands to Norway,
and in many other countries, teacher educators have been experimenting
with how to reorganize their programs to prepare their student teachers
for classroom practice.

This volume aims to provide teacher educators and researchers in
teacher education across the globe with an early sense of how the ideas
and approaches related to core practices are being taken up by universities
in different countries and contexts around the world. The institutional
efforts share common ground in their commitment to placing practice at
the center of their curriculum, but they differ in how they have defined
practice, which practices they have chosen to highlight, and how they
have integrated practice into their programs. The history of teacher education in each country also informs efforts to integrate practice more

centrally into teacher preparation. While the tension between theory and practice in professional education cuts across borders, each country has a different history of how it has navigated these tensions. Institutions must also contend with national policy and regulations, as well as local demands related to schools and the teacher workforce. The authors, who represent multiple European countries and Australia, delve into how work related to practice-based teacher education, with a particular focus on core practices, has been taken up across institutional and national contexts.

There are many ways of defining practice-based teacher education.[3] In this volume, we focus particularly on a version of practice-based teacher education that focuses on the teaching and learning of core practices during initial teacher preparation. We define core practices in teaching as those that are fundamental to teaching and grounded in disciplinary and pedagogical goals that teachers enact to support student learning.[4] Much of the early work on core practices focused on subject-specific practices or practices that are used across different subject matters, such as facilitating discussion. A related body of work on high-leverage practices identified nineteen practices that are conceptualized as the most important practices for novices to develop during preservice teacher education.[5] More recently, a number of scholars have been studying core practices that work toward more just and inclusive classrooms.[6]

An approach to teacher education grounded in core practices involves providing prospective teachers with the opportunity to analyze and enact complex practice aimed at ambitious learning. Grounded in sociocultural theory, this work recognizes the highly complex and contextual nature of teaching and the ways in which practice is always deeply connected to teachers' goals for student learning. Teacher educators must both identify the practices to target during professional education and also hone the pedagogies used to develop teachers' capacities to enact these practices. Although this approach identifies and specifies practices for prospective teachers to learn, such as facilitating classroom discussion or eliciting student thinking, the expectation is that novices will adapt these practices to their own contexts and students. The ultimate goal is not strict adherence to a small set of practices but rather adaptive expertise, in which teachers continue to refine, adapt, and iterate their practice over time.[7] A musical analogy might involve how musicians invest in learning a set of chords and scales, which then become the foundation for later improvisation.

It is important to acknowledge that research and professional preparation concerning particular practices of teaching has existed long before the concept of core practices appeared. For example, there is a long history of research on classroom discussion that includes work on dialogic teaching, accountable talk, uptake of student ideas, and other talk moves; this research cuts across subject matters and grade levels.[8] This body of work provides a deep understanding of the complexity of facilitating discussion that has informed the work of scholars who now identify this as a critical core practice. As this example illustrates, the identification of core practices relies on prior research, as well as professional consensus. A number of researchers have conducted versions of Delphi studies to engage teachers, teacher educators, and researchers in the process of identifying core practices in science, history, and project-based learning.[9] As noted earlier, other scholars are beginning to identify practices that are foundational to teaching for social justice.[10]

Another related line of research has to do with how to teach practices within the context of university-based teacher education. Researchers in this area emphasized the importance of moving from pedagogies of investigation in teacher education to pedagogies of enactment, in which prospective teachers are asked to enact elements of practice.[11] Grossman and her colleagues identified a framework for teaching practice that includes the importance of representations, decompositions, and approximations of practice. They argue that in learning a new practice, teachers need opportunities to see multiple examples of the practice, whether through video, model lessons, or classroom observation, and then to have the opportunity to see the distinct components that make up a more complex practice through decomposition. These decompositions allow teachers to develop "professional vision" and can target aspects of practice that can be developed and refined in approximations of practice, including rehearsals of practice, role-plays, simulations, and others.[12]

Based on this work, McDonald, Kazemi, and Kavanagh created a learning cycle that first introduces novice teachers to a practice through representations, often videos, which are analyzed and decomposed. Novices are then asked to enact the practice and reflect on their practice. A robust body of research has focused on one particular form of approximation—rehearsals of practice—building on the work of Magdalene Lampert, Elham Kazemi, Hala Ghousseini, and Megan Franke in mathematics.[13] Other forms of approximation also include role-plays, micro-teaching, and, increasingly, simulations, either live or virtual.[14] These approximations provide novices with the opportunity to try out new practices in an environment that is designed for professional learning and receive in-the-moment feedback, often with an opportunity to incorporate the feedback into subsequent attempts. Field placements also provide opportunities to see, enact, and reflect on practice. In some programs, student teachers first approximate a practice in their teacher education classroom and then are asked to try it out in their field placement. In others, cooperating teachers might be strong models of these practices for student teachers and can reflect on what it means to enact these practices.

Although many teacher educators and preparation programs have taken up the idea of core practices in their work, a number of scholars have also provided critiques of practice-based teacher education focusing on core practices. Scholars have critiqued this approach for its lack of attention to social justice and have raised concerns that the emphasis on practices signals a return to a more behavioral approach to teacher education, which has the potential to devalue teachers' knowledge and judgment.[15] Many of these researchers worry that focusing on core practices can simplify the complexity of teaching and limit the ability to improvise and adapt teaching for particular contexts. In a recent review of the literature on practice-based teacher education, Sarah Kavanagh responds to these critiques and clarifies that the theoretical underpinnings of this approach are explicitly sociocultural and the goal is not disembodied technique but rather practice that is deeply informed by knowledge, purpose, and values. As noted earlier, the original intent of an approach rooted in core practices is to provide a foundation for adaptive expertise, rather than insisting on fidelity. She goes on to argue that we need greater attention to practices that support justice-oriented goals. In this vein, some researchers have targeted practices that aim to address issues of equity, while others have introduced frameworks for practices that aim at more justice-oriented teaching.[16]

The focus on core practices in teacher education research and practice has developed significant momentum in the past decade. In addition to research and experimentation by teacher educators in their own classrooms, institutions have taken up the challenge of redesigning their entire program around this focus on a set of practices.[17] At the University of Connecticut, for example, Levine, Anagnostopoulos, and colleagues brought together faculty to identify a set of practices that could cut across the elementary teacher education program.[18] This effort involved significant discussion and negotiation among faculty members in the redesign process as faculty reoriented their teaching to focus on a set of practices.

Although the recent work specifically related to core and high-leverage practice began in the US, there has also been global uptake of this work, in countries all over the world. For example, at the Catholic University of Santiago, Chile, faculty have been working for a number of years to organize their teacher education program around the nineteen high-leverage practices identified by Deborah Ball and her colleagues.[19] As in the US, this work has involved bringing faculty together to determine which practices are most important for their prospective teachers to learn, to better prepare them for the classroom. A number of the chapters in this volume describe the redesign process of teacher education curriculum and practice in other national contexts as well.

In addition, there is a history of work related to the idea of core practices in other countries as well. One example is the work of the Swiss psychologist Hans Aebli, who specified a set of "forms of teaching," similar to the concept of core practices. He focused his work on the question of what elements of teaching a teacher must possess in order to understand, guide, and best support and sustain student learning. This work provides an interesting historical antecedent for the current discussion of foundational practices of teaching. Aebli's work is little known in non-German speaking countries but deserves greater recognition as an antecedent of the more recent efforts to identify foundational practices. Chapter 1 provides an introduction to Aebli's work and explores the relationship between his historical work on forms of teaching and the more recent work on core practices.

In chapter 2, Hanna Westbroek and her colleagues describe a practice-based teacher education program that explicitly addresses the motivational side of mastering core practices by making the program more *adaptive* to student teachers' general and personal learning needs. They describe a program at the Vrije Universiteit Amsterdam in which student teachers are offered a *learning sequence of core practices* that was designed by teacher educators in collaboration with mentors based at partnership schools, to ensure alignment between the university program and the typical learning trajectory student teachers experience at school. In addition, the development of core practices is adapted to the student teachers' own teaching practices and the goals that they aspire and connect to these practices, attending to the motivational aspects involved in learning new practices.

In chapter 3, Janette Bobis describes her efforts to redesign her teacher education classes in mathematics teaching around the core practices of eliciting, interpreting, and responding to students' thinking, facilitating classroom discussion, and providing prompts to differentiate student learning. In parallel to these refinements, she describes how she has revised her own pedagogies of practice—the strategies and approaches used to develop beginning teachers' understandings and effective enactment of these essential practices. Drawing on course documentation and preservice teachers' lesson plan data, Bobis explores how a research-informed instructional approach that focuses on challenging mathematics problems is implemented in the broader context of a practice-based initial teacher education program and provides readers with a deep understanding of the important role core practices play in teaching and learning mathematics through a student-centered problem-solving approach.

In chapter 4, Kirsti Klette, Inga Staal Jenset, and Gøril Brataas describe program redesign efforts from a secondary program in Norway and how the notion of core practices, together with the use of one specific observation protocol, supported with videos from K–12 classrooms, was used to strengthen teacher candidates' opportunity to enact practice during their professional training. The redesign work is set within a larger national effort to reform and strengthen teacher education in Norway. This chapter illustrates the role that practices codified as part of observation instruments can play in helping to develop a shared language for describing teaching and to provide a common tool for a teacher education program.

In chapter 5, Matthias Nückles and Marc Kleinknecht systematically address the important question of how university-based teacher education in Germany might foster the acquisition of certain core practices. Using the example of supporting self-regulated reading of texts, the authors investigate the extent to which student teachers in different settings acquire the ability to adaptively introduce their students to self-regulated text comprehension. By drawing on models of teacher professional development research, cognitive science, and educational psychology, among others, they are able to show the extent to which practicing a core practice in a small group of students has an impact on learning that practice.

In chapter 6, Alexander Gröschner, Susi Klaß, and Elisa Calcagni describe several initiatives in pre- and in-service teacher education that illustrate how teachers learn to enact core practices of productive classroom talk. They provide examples from recent studies in pre- and in-service teacher education seeking to promote these practices and their implications for teacher educators and researchers. For this purpose, they founded a "Learning to Teach-Lab: Science" as a learning environment to incorporate core practices in real and virtual classrooms at the University of Jena, Germany, using video as a tool to illustrate, reflect, and rehearse productive classroom talk. They illustrate the lab's great potential through their recent findings and connect it to core practices and practice-based teacher education.

In chapter 7, Kjersti Wæge, Janne Fauskanger, and Reidar Mosvold show how a practice-based approach is implemented in teacher education and professional development in Norway. Using the examples of rehearsal and co-enactment, they illustrate how basic core practices such as eliciting and responding, using representations, and pursuing goals can be understood and learned in cyclical processes. In various forms of rehearsal, the technique of time-out is successfully used, which allows for better understanding of student thinking in mathematical challenges, followed by collaborative reflection on procedures and effects when using different core practices.

Across these chapters, we see themes and variations in how the ideas related to core practices and practice-based teacher education have been picked up in different national contexts. In the concluding chapter, we return to some of these nuances and also address the questions raised by this work. Given some of the common challenges facing teacher educators across the world, we believe this volume will provide a more international perspective on the work related to practice-based teacher education and core practices, so that the field can better share and build knowledge across borders.

CHAPTER 1

Hans Aebli and His European Approach to Core Practices

Mediating Practical Abilities and Theoretical Understanding

Urban Fraefel and Kurt Reusser

INTRODUCTION

Although the concept of *core practices* as explored in this volume is relatively new, there are historical precedents in the work of Hans Aebli, a Swiss professor of cognitive and developmental psychology. Aebli's work is not well known beyond the German-speaking world, but within those regions he was recognized for his sophisticated framework for teacher education, which he presented in his 1961 book, *Basic Forms of Teaching*, and continued to refine throughout his career.[1] His approach to teacher education shares many similarities with core practices. Like current proponents of core practices, Aebli did not support the often-invoked opposition of theory and practice in teacher education. He also recognized early on the importance of practically tested yet theoretically grounded practices that enable teachers to initiate and promote thorough student learning.

Perhaps the most obvious convergence of Aebli's basic forms of teaching and core practices is that both approaches place challenging instructional components that are important to teachers and to learning success at the center of teacher education; this sets them apart from approaches that foreground theory prior to application, on the one hand, and a focus on simplistic drilling of narrow teaching techniques, on the other. Both also focus on practices, or forms of teaching, that are of a similar grain size. For example, Aebli identified basic forms of teaching such as "narrating/ presenting" and "demonstrating," which are analogous to practices such as "explaining and modeling content, practices, and strategies" that are mentioned in the context of core practices or high-leverage practices.[2] Both are roughly the same grain size and related to similar patterns of teacher activity that are essential for teaching and supporting student learning.

The underlying intention of this chapter is to introduce Aebli's approach to basic forms of teaching, which he scientifically founded and repeatedly improved on throughout his life, and to contrast it with the core practices approach. We first take a look at the fragile position of those who engaged in strengthening the practice-oriented aspects of teacher education, especially in Germany. Against this background, we describe the significance of Aebli's basic forms of teaching and trace their reception. Finally, we revisit in more depth commonalities and differences between the basic forms of teaching and core practices approaches with regard to their benefits in teacher education.

TOWARD PRACTICE-BASED TEACHER EDUCATION IN THE GERMAN-SPEAKING WORLD

To fully appreciate the significance of Aebli's work, it is important to understand the broad outlines of the role of practical training in teacher education in the German-speaking world. We limit our description to the German-speaking part of Europe, which constitutes the largest language area in Europe, because of significant variations in education systems and teacher education across European countries and even regionally within countries. Despite these variations, teacher education in Europe is largely in the hands of state institutions and regulated by the public administration.

In Germany, teacher education has for centuries been characterized by an ambivalence between a focus on the more theoretically oriented "Bildung" and the more practice-oriented "Ausbildung."[3] It is through an emphasis on Bildung that university students are supposed to acquire an academic habitus in addition to culturally significant content, while a focus on "Ausbildung" is considered preparation for a specific professional activity. According to Jürgen Oelkers, this tension is a typically German issue: "The dispute between non-purpose Bildung and professional training is epic, historically entrenched, and never resolved."[4]

While proponents of "Bildung" focus primarily on the development of the self—often with reference to humanistic ideals—those who advocate for professional "Ausbildung" put more emphasis on the ability to act effectively. This debate has also resonated in teacher education. "Bildung" has remained the guiding concept for teacher education, with a focus on foundational and theoretical knowledge as well as on development of the self, while the development of practical skills has hardly played a role at German universities and has been mostly outsourced to later professional learning ("learning on the job"). This is expressed, for example, in the statement of the German philosopher and educationalist Otto Bollnow: "Only in a period of theoretical preparation . . . can the conditions be created which enable the teacher to gain real experience in his later practical work."[5] Given the primacy of this view, proponents of practice-oriented teacher education have mostly found themselves in an outsider role. The largely theoretical preparatory course of study has remained characteristic of university teacher education in Germany to this day, and despite repeated criticism of its theoretical nature and remoteness from practice, the institutionally and structurally anchored dominance of academic teacher education underpinned by educational theory was not broken until late in the twentieth century.

Even the practice-oriented impulses of German reform pedagogy and its American equivalent, progressive education, found their way into the mainstream of public teaching practice only to a very limited extent.[6] Moreover, after the shock of World War II, German didactics was strongly shaped by self-critical questions of content and educational goals, while the focus on "how" and "by what means" was suspected of being merely a technological means to an end, of lacking sufficient analytical depth with regard to critical reflection on teaching subjects, and of doing little to contribute to society's educational mission of developing responsible citizens.[7] However, since the turn of the millennium, in parallel with international benchmark studies such as TIMSS and PISA, elements of practical education focused on acquiring skill in teaching have been introduced into the university phase of teacher education.[8] Furthermore, there are also signs that the focus of practical education is shifting from the drill-based introduction to a set of traditional teaching forms to a broad range of cognitively activating forms of teaching.

Aebli noted that practice has always had a low status in German teacher education, a state of affairs widely shared by practical education in Western cultures. He wrote that "practice in schools is considered primitive, regulated by low-level recipes and survival tactics."[9] Aebli himself held a very different opinion, believing that practice in schools that is not interpreted in a thoughtful and profound way would degenerate into routine or disappointment. Misguided attitudes such as resignation, cynicism, or escape into specialization would then creep in.[10]

German-speaking Switzerland, which is much less affected by ideological polarization, was only marginally impacted by the disputes over teacher education in Germany; the school system, and teacher education in particular, have remained comparatively practical for the most part and have been characterized by a focus on what is necessary and expedient to ensure a solid education of the upcoming generation. The pragmatic Swiss environment made it easier for Aebli to develop his ideas on teacher education and to help them resonate in practical teacher education.

AEBLI AS A FORERUNNER

Aebli's concern for psychologically based practices for teachers is reflected in his biography. After training as an elementary school teacher, he studied with Jean Piaget in Geneva and received his doctorate in 1951 with a highly regarded thesis, translated into several languages, in which he made Piaget's psychology applicable to teaching.[11] After a one-year study visit to the United States, he worked for ten years as a teacher educator in Zurich. During this time, he refined his "psychological didactics"—the title of his dissertation—and tested its key components in numerous design-based teacher training cycles.[12] In 1961, he published the results of his work under the title *Basic Forms of Teaching,* the main features of which are presented briefly in the next section. Because there is not enough space for a comprehensive presentation, we concentrate on central aspects that are significant for a comparison with the concept of core practices.[13]

To Think About Teaching Means to Focus on Students' Learning

The concern to which Hans Aebli was deeply committed is evident from the very first sentences of his dissertation, published in 1951: "How can a pupil be made to grasp this or that concept, process, or technique?" In line with Piaget's theory of mental development, Aebli's full interest was in the process of the acquisition of meaningful and flexible cognitive structures: "The 'matters' that exist outside the child's mind must become elements of his own thinking."[14] On this foundation, Aebli defined the task of didactics as "deriving from the psychological knowledge of the processes of mental formation those methodological measures which are most suitable for the development of the processes."[15] Aebli formulated this programmatic position at a time when behaviorism still dominated academic instructional psychology. In teacher education, the orientation of teaching toward the best possible student learning and understanding was hardly an issue at that time, as noted earlier. In German-speaking countries, including Switzerland, traditional and transmission-oriented teaching was predominant.

Drawing on Piaget's epistemological constructivism, Aebli considered it unrealistic to expect students to acquire meaningful concepts and understanding of contexts through instruction built primarily on mere passive perception and superficial activity without deep cognitive processing. He approached the question of the formation of knowledge structures and problem-solving abilities from two schools of thought: on the one hand, from the work of John Dewey, which Aebli studied intensively and which postulates a close interconnection of action and thought and the reflection on them, and on the other hand, from Piaget's structuralism and constructivism, according to which action schemata form the nucleus from which mental operations and concepts are constructed in the human mind. For Aebli, the connection between thinking and acting subsequently became a fundamental guiding principle; it is not for nothing that his main work in cognitive psychology is called "Thinking, the Ordering of Doing."[16]

For teaching, our best cognitive psychological knowledge of how people think and act may serve as a template for the mindful acquisition of concepts and mental structures in the process of schooling. "The essential features of the method to be followed in teaching are identical with those of reflection."[17] According to Aebli, it is only when teachers understand how people acquire something mentally that they can design instruction in such a way as to make deep and meaningful learning possible. Active and interested engagement with the subject matter, together with the adaptive support of the teacher, plays a crucial role. The trigger should be challenging problems and tasks that invite mindful action; carefully designed tasks that are deeply rooted in core ideas of disciplines are the raw materials for building cognitive structures.

Teachers as Scaffolds in Building Mental Structures   One of Aebli's central claims is that, without teacher support, the majority of students are unable to acquire sophisticated domain-specific concepts and structures completely on their own. He distanced himself from Piaget's thesis that cognitive development occurs quasi-lawfully by nature (i.e., without the substantial support of the social environment). Nevertheless, learners must always build their mental structures themselves, and no one can take the necessary effort away from them. However, to be successful with demanding tasks and content, they need the assistance of teachers and more capable peers who can provide adaptive support. Aebli rejected pure discovery learning without guidance. For most students, challenging learning without substantial guidance fails "as soon as the distance between the familiar schemata of thinking and a new operation exceeds a certain limit," a wording quite close to the description of Lev Vygotsky's zone of proximal development, though Aebli had no knowledge of Vygotsky's work at that time.[18] This was an early insight into the limitations of purely self-regulated learning, which, looking back at the discussions of the previous decades on this topic, should by now be undisputed.[19] It is noteworthy, however, that in contrast to what is sometimes suggested in the discussion of "constructivist learning environments," Aebli did not consider strong teacher support of learning activities to be at odds with his constructivist understanding of learning.[20]

The Twelve Basic Forms of Teaching   Aebli has been widely recognized among teachers for his *Basic Forms of Teaching*, still in print and translated into six languages, but not English.[21] For generations of teachers, especially in German-speaking countries, it has been a standard workbook for introducing teachers to professional teaching practice. Aebli succeeded in structuring central tasks and activities of the teacher in simple and comprehensible language and in providing instructions for their implementation. Just as important, he gave psychological rationales for how each activity supports students' learning processes.

Aebli's basic forms of teaching are based on two concerns: He wanted to give teachers adaptable tools to master important tasks of teaching. At the same time, he made it clear that such tools—the basic forms of teaching—must support student learning in the best possible way. These twin concerns are why Aebli's explanations of the basic forms always consist of two parts, one that introduces practical action and provides precisely described examples and another that explains the psychological basis for it, so that teachers understand what processes they trigger with it and how these contribute to student learning. The following summary is based on the 1983 edition of *Basic Forms of Teaching* (see also table 1.1).[22]

A first group comprises five basic forms by means of which the teacher brings the students into contact with a subject or content (i.e., provides the students with an experience). Aebli named five basic forms:

- *Narrating and presenting.* This is about how a teacher conveys information, gives input, and communicates in a way that is appropriate to the student.
- *Demonstrating.* This basic form means to demonstrate a skill or a working technique; in today's terminology, it largely corresponds to the concept of modeling.
- *Observing.* Here Aebli summarizes strategies in which the teacher brings students into contact with a wide variety of objects, has them observe phenomena closely, and illustrates content through

the use of media of all kinds to help students accurately grasp objects and form ideas.
- *Reading.* This basic form is about helping students in all subjects deal with texts—to understand, interpret, summarize, and use them.
- *Writing texts.* The teacher supports students in expressing themselves and communicating in writing. Students learn to compose texts, revise them, and test them for their effect.

A second group includes three basic forms that refer to *the planning and creation of learning sequences and respective learning environments* that enable (1) the understanding of complex actions, processes, and products; (2) the mental construction of abstract operations and strategies; and (3) the formation of content-specific conceptual structures. On the one hand, this group is about what students do when they are cognitively engaged in understanding new topics and the forms of thinking and acting associated with them. On the other hand, at the teacher's level, it is a matter of designing challenging tasks and learning situations to trigger and build higher-order forms of thinking and understanding with the necessary depth and quality.

These three basic forms aimed at building cognitive structures include the following:

- *Enabling grasping the structure of complex actions, processes or products.* The teacher sets a challenging goal and creates an environment in which the students become active in order to perform a course of action or a project task, or to understand the making of a product (e.g., a power plant, an aquarium, a family house, Swiss cheese). The teacher supports students in understanding the task and the steps necessary to perform an action or craft a product.
- *Fostering the buildup of abstract thinking operations.* The teacher identifies which thinking operations and strategies the mastery of an object or a discipline requires and that must be acquired. The teacher plans learning opportunities and supports students in engaging with a new disciplinary thinking skill, a content-specific

mental operation (i.e., rule-based processes or relations in mathematics or any other subject), looking at it from different angles, and adapting it to variable situations with increasing flexibility.

- *Assisting the acquisition of domain-specific concepts.* The teacher clarifies which concepts are to be acquired in this subject, what they comprise (e.g., visualized in a concept map), and what it takes for the students to acquire and enrich them.[23] The teacher supports the construction of elements of knowledge and of relationships necessary to understand the concept as a whole.

According to Aebli, it is not enough that the students are simply active externally; in his opinion, it is part of the teacher's responsibility to ensure that the mental operations necessary to grasp processes and objects and to build concepts are also carried out internally. These three basic forms are designed to help the teacher plan and guide instruction in such a way that the content will leave lasting traces on students' thinking processes over time.

The third group follows the course of a teaching-learning cycle that extends over a lesson or a series of lessons. Aebli argued that a certain sequence of phases, each with a specific function, is essential to ensure that students learn deeply and sustainably and build stable cognitive structures in the process. He also believed that teachers must have the tools and strategies necessary to implement and support these phases—socially and materially—in the classroom. Aebli characterized these four basic forms—and the role of teachers in their implementation—as follows:

- *Problem-triggered building up.* For students to build new mental structures requires their cognitive engagement, which is preferably to be achieved with challenging problems. Because students usually cannot solve the problems entirely on their own—Aebli rejected the concept of pure discovery learning—the teacher must be able to engage in *instructional dialogue* in order to provide students with minimal and appropriate prompts and information so that they can solve the problems. When problem-solving is done individually or in groups, *scaffolding* is used to support the process. Aebli took a cognitivist-constructivist position regarding the co-construction of knowledge; a sociocultural perspective that favors more participatory forms of conversation had not yet been developed at that time.[24]

- *Working through.* By this necessary step in the acquisition of deep knowledge, Aebli meant that students need to achieve a solid understanding of the new things they are confronted with in order to create flexibility with regard to its use in new situations. Here the role of the teacher is to guide what today also is called *deliberate practice.*[25] Because newly acquired concepts often remain elusive until they have been thoroughly worked through in different contexts, the teacher guides the working through (which the students are usually not yet able to do independently) by setting varying tasks and confronting students with phenomena that are slightly different from the original learning situation and that need to be grasped in their underlying structure, as well as by actively supporting students as needed.
- *Rehearsing and practicing.* With this basic form, the teacher ensures that learning content—action patterns, procedures, strategies, but also facts and figures, vocabulary—is automated, internalized, and stabilized through repeated completion. Aebli also viewed the teacher's task as *enabling success and motivating for perfection.* This may be an aspect of teaching skills that has lost priority in some areas today but is essential for building expertise.
- *Applying.* This basic form amounts to the teacher creating problem situations in which students must, largely without the teacher's help, apply previously acquired and consolidated competencies in new contexts. Aebli refers in particular to working in groups, including the acquisition of skills necessary for self-regulated learning.[26]

The challenge for the teacher is to ensure that all students, not just the particularly interested and gifted ones, go through these stages of an integral learning cycle. Therefore, it is quite possible to speak of a phase model for teaching that aims at a complete learning cycle, starting from the first

TABLE 1.1 *Overview of the basic forms of teaching listed by Aebli*

DOMAIN	BASIC FORM OF TEACHING	THE TEACHER . . .
Providing the students with an experience	Narrating and presenting	conveys information, gives input, and communicates in a way that is appropriate to the student.
	Demonstrating	demonstrates a skill or a working technique; in today's terminology, it corresponds to the concept of modeling.
	Observing	brings students into contact with objects through the use of media of all kinds to help students accurately grasp objects and form ideas.
	Reading	helps students in all subjects deal with texts—to understand, interpret, summarize, and use them.
	Writing texts	supports students in expressing themselves and communicating in writing.
Planning learning environments to construct conceptual knowledge and thinking operations	Enabling grasping actions and processes	plans challenging situations in which students take action to solve a problem or understand a process or product.
	Fostering the buildup of thinking operations	plans opportunities for students to build new mental operations and master them with increasing flexibility.
	Assisting the acquisition of concepts	clarifies which concepts need to be acquired in this subject and what it takes to grasp and deepen their structure.
Enabling complete learning cycles	Problem-triggered building up	initiates learning processes with challenging problems, engages in instructional dialogue, and provides students with appropriate information to solve the problems.
	Working through	guides deliberate practice to stabilize elusive new concepts by setting tasks slightly different from the original ones and supports actively where needed.
	Rehearsing and practicing	ensures that content is automated and internalized through repeated completion; enables success and motivates for perfection.
	Applying	creates situations in which students must, largely without the teacher's help, apply previously acquired and consolidated competencies in new contexts.

Source: Based on Hans Aebli, *Zwölf Grundformen des Lernens: Eine Allgemeine Didaktik auf psychologischer Grundlage* (Stuttgart: Klett, 1983). Some terms are linguistically adapted to current terminologies.

encounter with the problem, through deep understanding and rehearsal, to its application and transfer to other areas. Put another way, if the teacher allows one or more of these stages to be left out, sustained learning is uncertain or even fails entirely.

The Inner Structure of Aebli's Basic Forms of Teaching   Aebli's goal was not to provide (prospective) teachers with narrowly defined patterns for dealing with classroom situations in a recipe-like manner but rather to enable teachers to perceive and consciously shape student learning processes while teaching. He argued that teachers who are not prepared to focus on the quality of student learning, and who do not understand how learning unfolds, are unlikely to be able to support student learning. If teachers don't understand what's going on in students' heads, according to Aebli, it will be the students who suffer the consequences.

At this point, it is important to mention that Aebli introduced the distinction between a *surface structure* and a *deep structure*, which he borrowed from Chomskian linguistics and adapted for his concept of basic forms.[27] According to Aebli, the surface structure comprises the visible actions of instruction, while the deep structure is the synchronously unfolding cognitive processes of the learners. Since Aebli adopted the model of surface and deep structure for instructional psychology, it has become a central conceptual framework in the German-speaking world, especially in instructional research, where it has proved particularly fruitful.[28]

For Aebli, it is indispensable to link these two levels: the visible teaching structure (the surface structure) must also have the deeper learning level in view; and conversely, the learning processes must be set in motion, supported, and consolidated by actions on the visual level. For example, in the basic form of "problem-triggered building up," both the underlying process of initiating learning through action *and* the most appropriate instructional arrangements and interactions at the visual level are of interest. Therefore, for each basic form, Aebli described a set of teacher activities—the surface structure—and explored what the learning opportunities for students triggered by these activities are and how students' thinking could unfold by means of the support of the teacher—in other words, what takes place on the deep structural level. Thus, the basic forms are carefully chosen, on the one hand, based on the concrete activities the teacher has to deal with in the classroom and, on the other hand, based on the forms' potential for deep structural learning. In this way, each basic form is a manageable unit that describes these two levels of pedagogical challenge.

Aebli reworked the basic forms several times, on the one hand to react to the changing requirements of teaching and on the other hand to keep the basic forms up to date with the knowledge of the time on cognition, learning and teaching. Today, against the backdrop of social and educational change and expanded understanding of individual and social knowledge construction, the basic forms that Aebli formulated in the 1960s would certainly be described differently. For example, social constructivist interpretations of dialogic classroom discussions would be given more weight, and learning support would be described using today's terminology (e.g., formative assessment, diagnosis, individual goal setting, feedback). We can also identify areas that were not considered essential practices by Aebli, largely because of the era in which he was working. For example, it is fair to say that Aebli did not give the cooperative aspects and social learning in the classroom the importance that they have today.

To sum up, all basic forms proposed by Aebli have some common features: they have a practical significance for the teacher and prove to be necessary components of teaching; they support student thinking and promote sustained learning; and their use is explained in detail, mostly with examples.

Aebli understood his basic forms of teaching not as a static compendium that conclusively names firmly defined practices but as a dynamic concept that is (1) oriented to the necessities of a given learning culture and the needs of teachers and learners and (2) rooted in a growing understanding of how learning processes take place and how they can be supported in productive ways. In addition, Aebli also provided suggestions for how teachers can learn these basic forms and enact them adaptively in different contexts. We will come back to this last point later.

"BASIC FORMS OF TEACHING" AND "CORE PRACTICES"

We pointed out at the beginning of the chapter the remarkable fact that, born of the same intentions, the basic forms of teaching and core practices approaches have many commonalities despite emerging in completely different cultural and temporal contexts. Having discussed Aebli's basic forms of teaching and the environment in which the approach was conceived, we can now identify these commonalities in more detail. The approaches that foreground both the basic forms of teaching and core practices developed out of a perceived shortcoming of teacher education programs—namely, the inadequate preparation of student teachers for their practical and crucial task of providing the best possible support for student learning. Scholars in both approaches seek to overcome the separation in teacher education between the acquisition of theoretical knowledge and engagement in practice by providing student teachers with access to complex but manageable instructional components that are theoretically supported and practically effective. Both approaches describe manageable clusters of teacher actions that are indispensable for mastering a particular teaching challenge and view as the overriding goal that such teacher practices should initiate and support deep and sustained learning and understanding in students. Scholars in both traditions see these basic forms or core practices as based on knowledge of educational psychology, learning, and instruction, and made learnable for teachers so they can best support students in their progress. The goal of both approaches is to introduce prospective teachers to professional and flexible practices for their teaching activities and to emphasize the adaptive use of these strategies both in classroom instruction and in supporting groups and individual students. Finally, scholars in both traditions address the question of *how* to build and consolidate such practices in teacher education and tackle the work of both teacher educators and student teachers at all levels.

Along with these commonalities, there are also significant differences that cannot be explained by the different contexts in which they emerged. Certainly, also due to the era, the theoretical background of the two concepts is different. Aebli was a cognitive psychologist who was influenced by his collaboration with Piaget, with whom Aebli shared the basic constructivist stance, and thus he clearly set himself apart from the behaviorist mainstream of the time. However, Aebli also rejected Piaget's stage model of mental development and emphasized the social construction of knowledge and cognition, and especially the role of the teacher in these learning processes, as made clear by the following passage:

> The teacher stimulates learning processes by designing a structured learning environment, and he guides the child to build structures of behavior and thinking with which he is familiar as a member of a given culture. In this way, the child is socialized, that is, the child acquires the cultural techniques, affective possibilities, and attitudes that are alive in his or her sociocultural environment.[29]

Here Aebli hints at the sociocultural concepts that fully underpin today's core practices movement. Specifically, the proponents of core practices believe that individual development and learning cannot be understood without referencing the social context in which they are embedded. This refers both to teachers, who must understand themselves as part of the society and, particularly, of the profession whose practices they represent, and to their work with students, whose skills in social interaction and co-constructive learning teachers are fostering.

STRATEGIES IN TEACHER EDUCATION

We turn now to the strategies teacher education can use to promote the development of sophisticated practices on the part of prospective teachers. Grossman and colleagues pointed out that "there is relatively little theory that informs the actual pedagogy of professional education, because this has not been the focus of many classic studies of professional education and socialization."[30] For core practices, however, there is a framework that has inspired much research and development. Grossman and her colleagues proposed a three-step process for building practices in teacher education courses:

> *Representations* of practice comprise the different ways that practice is represented in professional education and what these various representations make visible to novices. *Decomposition* of practice involves breaking down practice into its constituent parts for the purposes of

teaching and learning. *Approximations* of practice refer to opportunities for novices to engage in practices that are more or less proximal to the practices of a profession.[31]

This process aims to bring prospective teachers' actual practices closer to the desired practices of the profession, and as such, it is appropriate from a sociocultural perspective. Other scholars identified the use of a learning cycle as a preferred form in which prospective teachers go through the three steps outlined above in repeated cycles in order for them to learn to enact core practices.[32]

Aebli's method had an analogous orientation in that the basic forms of teaching were modeled, tested in practice, and then analyzed, primarily, according to Aebli's approach, from the perspective of cognitive psychology of learning, in order to draw consequences for the teaching of student teachers. His core idea, which he himself practiced for over a decade as a teacher educator, was the combination of training sessions, theoretical inputs, and teaching in schools that are specifically established for this purpose as part of the teacher education college or university.[33]

Among other things, Aebli advocated for so-called instructional rehearsal courses in teacher education. The concept of an instructional rehearsal course has been adopted by many schools of education and, especially along with the use of video, has paved the way for newer rehearsal formats of teacher education. In terms of content, such courses usually followed Aebli's basic forms of teaching, which were worked on and deepened in cycles. In terms of method, in addition to discussions in the courses and teaching in the assigned classes, the rehearsals used microteaching, which was one of the most innovative forms of practicing teaching at the time. In practica that were held in parallel to the instructional rehearsals, connections were made to real-world teaching situations in all their complexity.[34]

Aebli's body of work demonstrates his clear commitment to teacher education that consistently bridges theory and practice. In addition to his bestselling *Twelve Basic Forms of Teaching*, which has been widely popular among professionals in German-speaking countries, his thoughts about teacher education settings, which come close to our current understanding of cognitive apprenticeship, had a strong resonance in Switzerland.[35]

If Aebli were alive today, it is safe to assume that he would have welcomed and used technical advances available, such as using videos for modeling and practicing basic forms. Here, too, there is a similarity with the learning cycles that are used to build up core practices.[36]

CONCLUSION

Despite obvious differences in the emergence and theoretical position of the Aebli's basic forms of teaching and today's core practices, their commonalities are striking in terms of their intentions, their manifestations, their function in the education of future teachers, and their forms of rehearsal. Therefore, we argue that Aebli's approach deserves to be recognized as a forerunner of what is now known as the core practices approach in the German-speaking world.

Hans Aebli had the distinction of being the first in the German-speaking world to consistently interpret the practices of teachers from the mental processes of learners, with the goal of supporting students' learning in the best possible way. He designed forms of teaching that are both theoretically informed and practice-oriented, and made a decisive and lasting contribution, especially in German-speaking countries, to improving the quality and impact of teaching. From today's perspective, Aebli's achievements in cognitive psychology, teaching and learning, and teacher education were groundbreaking, and it is still worthwhile today to be inspired by the central messages of his work.

CHAPTER 2

A Motivational Perspective on Learning Core Practices

The Case of a Dutch Teacher Education Program

Hanna Westbroek, Anna Kaal, and Sebastiaan Dönszelmann

INTRODUCTION

Meet Nicole. After earning her master's degree in geography, she decided to do a one-year teacher training program at Vrije Universiteit Amsterdam. She is now four months into the program. She feels at home at her internship school: her students seem to accept her authority, she is able to explain the subject matter well, and students have friendly chats with her. Nicole generally provides instruction, has students do assignments while she walks around and answers questions, and then the entire class discusses the assignments. On Mondays, Nicole visits the teacher training institute for pedagogical courses, which currently focus on the core practice of "making learning visible." Her school mentor has challenged her to experiment with this, but Nicole worries. How can you gain more insight into learning and give students more responsibility while at the same time remaining in charge? She feels she needs to change her repertoire considerably, while she has only just started to master basic teaching skills. What will happen if she asks students all kinds of questions and has them respond to each

other? Will the working atmosphere change? And will her students
learn to master the compulsory material sufficiently?

Nicole's example is representative of many student teachers who participate in our teaching education (TE) program. This is a one-year post–
master's degree program for academic teachers of most school subjects
(science, languages, humanities) who are to work in higher general or pre-
university education. All student teachers have previously obtained a
master's degree in the subject area they are going to teach in. After three
to four months, many of them shift their focus from a self-centered "sur-
viving the classroom" state of mind to a more engaged focus on student
needs. In this chapter, we will illustrate how our TE program is geared to
adapt to this shift and to the students' learning needs. We will look at
Nicole at different stages in her development as a beginning teacher to
illustrate key characteristics of our practice-based teacher education (PBTE)
program. Our aim is to explain the design choices we made, to share our
experience with core practices (CP) and to present our dreams for the
future.

   We developed our curriculum in 2015 from the felt need to strengthen
the connection between educational theory and practice and to explicitly
address *motivational aspects* of mastering CP. Our old curriculum was
designed to reflect different teacher roles (the teacher as performer, designer,
educator, and professional) with each role being explored in separate course
blocks. We inserted CPs into our new curriculum, such as "starting your
class" or "promoting learning processes," to do more justice to the inte-
grative nature of teacher competencies. We wanted to blend knowledge
development and skills development in such a way that student teachers
not only want to learn *about* CPs but also are motivated to engage in a
meaningful deliberate practice.[1]

   We designed two complementary courses that provide student teachers with opportunities to encounter, explicate, and examine personal *learning needs*. In many PBTE approaches, the assumption seems to be that
student teachers automatically develop learning intentions when offered
sufficient opportunities and support.[2] The first, a general skills course (section 3), offers a learning sequence of CPs based on an analysis of the

typical needs of beginning student teachers. A blended learning approach enables student teachers to make personal choices at the moment learning needs present themselves during their internship to create a "just-in-time" experience. Student teachers also have the opportunity to explore and revisit the CPs when deemed necessary.

The second course (section 4) is offered three months into the program, when student teachers generally enter a phase of relative stagnation. Like Nicole, they start to feel in control in lessons that are predominantly teacher-centered. Although they acknowledge the value of more learner-centered approaches, they are hesitant to change. To create a tipping point, we designed a course that centers on student teachers' current teaching practices and personal theories and concerns as a starting point for reflection on what they have accomplished and how to continue from there.

In the following sections, we will follow Nicole and how she experiences her trajectory as a student teacher at the Vrije Universiteit Amsterdam (VU), at the start of her program (section 3), after three months (section 4), and at the end of the year (conclusion). We will present insights from course evaluations and additional focus group interviews to further illustrate our student teachers' experiences. We conclude this chapter with a reflection on how a focus on learning needs contributes to insight into the motivational side of developing CPs. First, we will further unpack the ideas that guided the design.

THEORETICAL UNDERPINNING OF THE PROGRAM

Our starting point is a situated perspective on learning how to teach—that is, cognition is situated in particular physical and social contexts, social and personal in nature, and distributed.[3] Learning needs cannot emerge from experience alone but emerge from insight through feedback on one's functioning in practice, paired with existing knowledge about alternative approaches to "good teaching" (top-down).[4] Such a top-down reference is needed to widen student teachers' perspectives beyond their own experience. It should as much as possible connect to the development phases and learning needs of the student teacher to be meaningful.[5] In order to make knowledgeable, meaningful decisions about developing new repertoire, reflection and, following from that, deliberate practice should occur mostly in collaboration with peers, school mentors, and teacher educators. This focus on the development of learning needs contributes to the education of teachers as adaptive and responsible professionals, who are able to use insights from research to underpin and develop their teaching practice, thereby increasingly implementing principles of ambitious teaching.[6]

Besides this situated perspective, the concept of "practical usefulness" explicitly guided our design. New practices are perceived as useful by student teachers only if they are evaluated as sufficiently (1) *congruent* (not conflicting with important goals), (2) *instrumental* (procedures are available that show how to implement a new practice in one's own context), and (3) *low cost* (positive effects outweigh the effort to change).[7] In general, what we perceive as "practically useful" is largely determined by the possibilities of the context we work in. Most Dutch secondary school teachers, for example, teach groups of twenty-five to thirty students who do not participate in the class voluntarily; they need to cover mandatory content within a given time frame; and so on. In such contexts, not everything is possible.[8] Decisions about teaching practices will therefore never be optimal for the learning processes of *all* students in a classroom. Teachers simply have to weigh too many important but conflicting goals simultaneously.[9]

A central tool in the second course is *goal system representations* (GSRs). GSRs are representative images of teaching practices that student teachers have developed, given their complex learning context. They show how lessons tend to unfold as a sequence of "building blocks" or "modules," which efforts teachers take to design each lesson module, and how these modules are connected to personal goals (we discuss an example in the section "Student Teachers Reflect on Their Goal System Representation"). Goals are defined as personal constructs that represent *desired states* and have proved to be the most proximate determinant for action.[10] Goals in a GSR can typically reflect principles of teaching (e.g., "activate prior knowledge") fundamental beliefs about teaching ("students need to become scientifically literate"), and constraints that emerge from the work context ("create work order"). Finally, GSRs can be seen as a teacher's "personal theory" about teaching practice.[11] GSRs are not static but develop over time and can differ by context.

A GSR can help student teachers to understand how *new* CPs relate to their current teaching practice and to find ways to implement these practices through *modular redesign*.[12] Modular redesign starts from the notion that your GSR represents what you have already accomplished. The lesson modules that represent your repertoire form the materials you can work with. You can recombine and adapt these modules as much as you like—for example, to incorporate activities that make learning visible. This allows student teachers to assess more easily how such adaptations may affect their goals and estimate which adaptation they feel comfortable with. This way, modular redesign contributes to revealing the potential of new practices and to motivating student teachers to experiment with new CPs.

In the next two sections we illustrate how our design adopted this motivational perspective on mastering CPs.

A LEARNING SEQUENCE OF CORE PRACTICES

Four weeks into the program. Nicole has just come out of an intervision meeting in which students reflect on challenges they encounter at their internships. Feedback from her peers has made her realize that she has difficulty confronting students. She is afraid confrontation will undermine a good relationship. On entering the program, Nicole hardly had any teaching experience. Because she occasionally tutored, she had some insight into the content of the school subject of geography. Her image of a "good teacher" was shaped by her own experiences as a student. During the online module and the following discussion on one of the first CPs, "making contact," Nicole became aware that her behavior is pivotal for making her pupils feel seen and heard. At her internship school, she observed other teachers' behavior, and her school mentor soon encouraged her to teach parts of classes. She has now quickly learned her students' names and enjoys having conversations with them; she tries to show them how she values their input. Today, however, she has realized that there is more to building relationships than simply creating a positive atmosphere, and she has decided to experiment with different types of leadership behavior in class. She knows the CP of "managing the class" will be dealt with at the institute in a few weeks' time, but the online module and assignments have already been made available, and she is able to delve into the topic and is excited to get started on her learning question.

The backbone of our first course design is a learning sequence of CPs codesigned by VU teacher educators and school mentors of partner schools. Nicole's case illustrates how from the start of the program, student teachers are supported to examine their learning needs and develop educational behaviors in their zone of proximal development. By exploring different CPs theoretically and practically, together with peers, her school mentor, and VU teacher educators, Nicole is able to mirror her practice and the dilemmas she encounters and gradually acquires a deeper understanding.

The CPs are as much as possible adapted to general developmental phases and typical concerns of student teachers (table 2.1).[13] The first phase of the program concerns the skills a teacher needs to design and enact a lesson that meets basic criteria such as designing clear learning goals and creating and maintaining work order. CPs that belong to this phase include making contact with students and providing clear and complete instruction. The focus is merely on "the self," as beginning student teachers often struggle with adopting the role of the teacher and director of the teaching-learning process. The CPs offered in the second phase explicitly address enhancing learning processes by making learning visible, providing productive feedback, and managing positive group dynamics. At this stage, student teachers tend to shift to a more engaged focus on their student group, although they are often hesitant to implement more learner-centered practices. In the third phase, the perspective is broadened toward enhancing *individual* learning processes and stimulating personal growth of students. CPs such as differentiated instruction are now the focus of the program.

For each CP, student teachers are invited to work through an online module using educational videos (Edu clips) and accompanying literature. In the module, the CP is explained, exemplified, modeled, and connected

TABLE 2.1 *Overview of the learning sequence of core practices: Phase I (the first 3 months), phase II (3–6 months), and phase III (the final 6 months)*

Phase I	1	Making contact
	2	Starting class
	3	Building and spending credit
	4	Preparing class
	5	Keeping order
	6	Providing instruction and finishing class
Phase II	7	Seeing your pupils
	8	Enhancing learning
	9	Making learning visible
	10	Leading
	11	Creating a safe atmosphere
	12	Testing learning
Phase III	13	Designing learning sequences
	14	Getting to know adolescents
	15	Taking into account behavioral and learner characteristics
	16	Systematically evaluating your teaching
	17	Dealing with diversity
	18	Differentiating within the group
	19	Giving responsibility
	20	Being a mentor
	21	Using your professional space

to theory; often, practical assignments are suggested. The main purpose of the online module is that student teachers relate the CP to their school mentor's practice or their own practice. Nicole, for example, learned that her behavior toward her students contributed to a basic need of students to feel connected.[14] The CPs are then further modeled, practiced, and discussed in sessions at the institute (a new CP every one to two weeks). Together, student teachers reflect on experiences and connect these to theoretical frameworks in order to come to a broader common understanding of the CP and to develop a common language. We contend that such broader, theoretical understanding is necessary for a proper examination of learning needs. Nicole, for example, became aware of different interpersonal teacher behavior this way.[15] She also learned more about herself and

FIGURE 2.1 *The pedagogical components of the general course. The sequence of core practices is offered in a blended approach. CPs are explained, exemplified, modeled, and connected to theory in scheduled sessions, and student teachers are offered personalized opportunities to rehearse and reflect on their experiences at the Vrije Universiteit Amsterdam (with peers and teacher educators) as well as at their internship (with the school mentor). The student teachers' learning needs are central to the process.*

why she had difficulty with "confrontational" behavior, which fed her desire to experiment with leadership.

Because the CPs reflect basic teacher developmental stages, our student teachers often experience a match between the CP learning sequence offered and their experiences in their internship. However, the online modules also allow a blended approach to the learning cycle, catering to different learning needs and autonomous choices with respect to what student teachers want to focus on and when and how they want to do so (as Nicole does for the CP "managing the class").

At the institute, peer feedback sessions and sessions focused on specific subject instruction (e.g., foreign languages) always allow room for further exploration, rehearsal, and individual questions that arise. In peer feedback sessions, different reflection strategies are explained and practiced, the purpose being that student teachers learn together and develop reflection tools that will continue to support them throughout their professional careers. Student teachers are also supported to rehearse (aspects of) CPs in their internships. The school mentors have access to the program and online modules and are informed by the institute when a new CP is being introduced.

Recent evaluations of the approach in 2022 (surveys, $n = 43/48$ total) and structured focus group interviews (two hours, after finishing phase II or phase III, one group of three student teachers and three groups of two) show that student teachers recognize and positively value its adaptive features. A student teacher remarked, "What I really like about the phases as we have gone through them is that every time I notice that I want to do something different in my lesson, or that I want to go a step further, that [new practice] is discussed." Another student teacher relates how the CPs provided a helpful frame of reference for "good teaching": "When you see 'making contact' in the overview you don't immediately think you can already do that; you are just starting out and there really are aspects you don't know about yet." Some student teachers link this to the development of their professional identity: "When you reach the phase in which you start to think about the kind of teacher you want to be, the CP of 'seeing your pupils' really fits." The sequencing only seemed to feel "off" for the CP "testing learning," which forms an important part of the final test at the end of phase II and is also introduced in the sequence at the end of phase II. The possible blend between guided learning at the institute (a chronological approach) and self-study in the modules (less bound in time) may sometimes require teacher educators to direct students toward an online module that they are not yet aware of.

The student teachers appreciate the connection made between theory and practice, for example in the sessions at the institute: "Those workshops were very instructive, because you actually put the theory you have been working on, or parts of it, into practice together with a small group of peers. Everyone was very happy with that!" They also recognize that the blended approach leaves room for individual choices: "Sometimes I wanted to go back and pick up some extra literature. It was nice to have all those modules online, so you could return and see what it [*the CP*] was all about."

Further critical comments include that the content of the sessions at the institute repeat too much of the Edu clips and that the online modules require a lot of preparation. Some suggested that a more differentiated approach would be valuable during the live sessions; our program participants include student teachers studying in bachelor's degree programs (minors), student teachers who have recently or not so recently finished their master's degree, and student teachers who have embarked on a new career at a later age.

The student teachers' evaluation of the link between CPs and the internship vary and seems to depend on the structure provided by the school mentor: "I was given a lot of freedom. I had to proactively ask for specific feedback on [CPs]. Nothing wrong with that, but sometimes it also felt I was left to my own devices." Another student teacher had a more positive experience: "My school mentor was taking a pedagogical coaching course herself and applied rubrics and video fragments to coach me. When you are all learning at the same time then you are all enthusiastic and motivated!"

We will return to the evaluation of the approach in the conclusion.

STUDENT TEACHERS REFLECT ON THEIR
GOAL SYSTEM REPRESENTATION

Let us return to Nicole after three months of theory and practice. She is now teaching her school mentor's complete fourth-grade geography classes (two hours per week). She is well supervised, but she also experiences stress because of the many new responsibilities. She wants to do the right thing for her students. Her lessons have a straightforward structure: discuss homework, provide instructions; students complete assignments, assignments are discussed in class. Her relationship with the students and the working atmosphere are usually good; she usually knows how to maintain their attention, and she is able to get them to work. At times, she wonders whether students truly understand the study material. Could there be room for improvement? Is this really the way she wants to teach? At the same time, she manages to keep up with the program and the students, and her school mentor seem satisfied. This gives her peace of mind: Why change things?

After about three months of training, many student teachers come to terms with the basics of managing their class, which usually includes a classical class structure. Student teachers who still experience difficulties usually remain focused on implementing CPs that concern "order." Student teachers who are able to lead their group are, like Nicole, usually quite satisfied with their approach, as are their mentors and pupils. As a result, they are often given more responsibilities at their internship schools; at the same time, they may experience more stress. This combination generally means that student teachers become less open to expanding their pedagogical repertoire with new CPs that are, for example, focused on actively involving students in class and that require more of a coaching role from the teacher.[16] Frequently, external reasons are given for not experimenting with new perspectives, such as "my students are not ready yet." The challenge for our TE program is to motivate student teachers to keep on investigating their teaching practice. The second course, "reflection on your goal system representation," was designed to create a tipping point and challenges student teachers to consider their teaching practice from a broader perspective, to explicate their personal theories, and to formulate their learning needs.

In the course, student teachers individually construct a visual image that represents how their lessons generally tend to unfold, resulting in a goal system representation. They are asked to think of the separate building blocks or modules that make up their lessons and write each of them on a separate Post-it (the "what" row). To this sequence of "building blocks," the student teachers add the efforts they take to design each of these modules (the "how" row). Subsequently, the student teachers connect the different modules to the different goals they try to achieve with them: Why do they think the module is important? Each goal is again written on a separate Post-it. Student teachers are encouraged to consider for each goal whether there might be a higher goal connected to it; this way, different layers of goals may emerge (the "why" rows), resulting in goals that reflect deeper perceptions and a teacher's vision or personal theory about teaching. Finally, student teachers are asked to assess all their lesson modules and goals as positive (+), negative (–), or unclear (?), and to think of possible points for further development. This method has been applied in studies on teachers' GSRs.[17] It forms the starting point for a reflection process.[18]

Nicole's GSR is pictured in figure 2.2. She typically starts her lesson by greeting her students. She then introduces a quote or image that reflects the topic; she explains the topic and new subject matter, after which her students work on tasks. She ends her lesson with a reflection on the learning goals (the "what" row). To prepare the part of the class in which she explains subject matter, Nicole typically creates a guiding PowerPoint presentation based on her school mentor's presentation

FIGURE 2.2 *Nicole's goal system representation.*

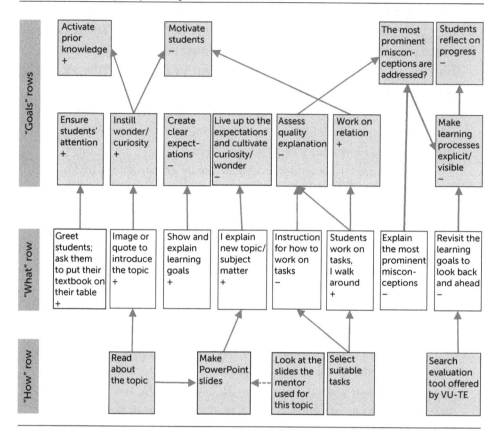

(the "how" row). An important goal for Nicole is to make learning visible, in order to reach a higher goal: that students are able to reflect on their learning process (the "why" row). This is the reason she revisits the learning goals at the end of the lesson. While assessing the different ingredients in her GSR, Nicole realized that she is quite satisfied with parts of her lesson (+ assessments). She, however, does not know whether she has been able to address the most important misconceptions (?–assessment). She is not satisfied with the end of her lesson (–assessment). She feels that merely asking students to raise their hands if they think they have achieved the goals does not come close to sufficiently making learning visible, let alone to her students' reflecting on their progress.

After creating their GSRs and discussing them, student teachers tend to develop a deeper understanding of what they are already capable of and what might be developmental points. In this way, GSRs form the starting point for self-evaluation and for modular redesign. In the course student teachers additionally discuss literature dealing with highly ambitious CPs that are becoming relevant to them at this stage, such as "formative evaluation and providing productive feedback" and "ways to enhance student autonomy and responsibility." These are also part of the general CP learning sequence (see section "A Learning Sequence of Core Practices"). Like Nicole, many student teachers realize at this point that formative evaluation is made up of different activities that each have different goals, for themselves *and* for their students. Student teachers often realize that such activities may help their students to develop self-insight, which is a condition for differentiated instruction and CPs that support student autonomy. The literature that is discussed elaborates not only on the underlying rationales but also on the conditions and design guidelines necessary to implement this type of CP.

Once student teachers have developed a common understanding of the CPs that are discussed in the literature, they are asked to reflect on the CPs' *practicality*. The student teachers are invited to discuss how they would like to *recombine and adapt* their lesson modules in order to stepwise incorporate principles of highly ambitious CPs (*modular redesign*).[19] The student teachers are also asked whether the changes in their GSR add new goals or whether previous goals may be achieved more successfully. This invites student teachers to incorporate a new CP in a way that they feel comfortable with, fitting the goals they would like to achieve. These reflective discussions tend to lead to the formulation of specific intentions and expectations, including new behaviors student teachers want to rehearse. Finally, we ask student teachers to think about how they can check these expectations: What information could they collect in their classes to evaluate the changes they made?

FIGURE 2.3 *Nicole's adapted goal system representation. The gray boxes and arrows show what Nicole changed and which goals she feels will improve.*

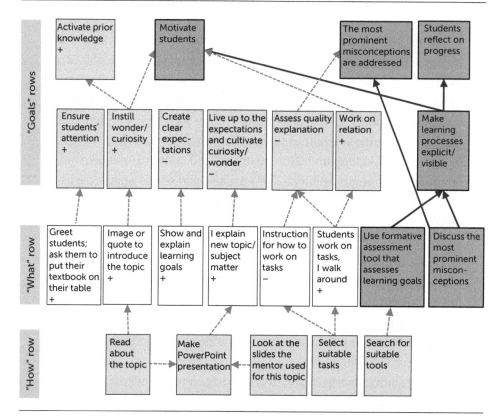

Figure 2.3 represents Nicole's adapted version of her GSR. She was one of the students who wanted to work on formative evaluation practices. From the readings and discussions, she has learned how well-designed questions can reveal commonly held misconceptions, facilitating "analysis of student responses." She has also realized how this can form a starting point for a class discussion. She has acquired a deeper understanding of the importance of letting students discuss their ideas and how valuing their input can contribute to a feeling of connection. Creating a safe environment for students to express themselves is essential for all this to work. As a first step, Nicole incorporates a formative

assessment activity at the end of her lesson. She has decided that fast feedback (FF) is a practically useful strategy to do this, as this is a quick and still pretty much teacher-led formative type of activity that engages all students. In an FF activity, the teacher poses a conceptual question to all students that is geared at a typical conceptual mistake that students make with the topic at hand. The students are offered a format for answering that makes their answers directly visible to the teacher (e.g., drawing; multiple choice). This way, the phase of analyzing student responses on the spot is simplified for the teacher.[20] She will discuss the results of the FF activity with her students afterward. She believes that this will help her achieve the goal of making learning processes visible to her students; she knows this is a condition for students reflecting on their learning processes (a higher goal) and for ultimately strengthening their motivation. She feels somewhat insecure about "discussing the most prominent misconceptions," as she now wants to try a more interactive way. Her teacher educator supports her to stepwise rehearse stimulating her students to react to each other's input. Nicole realizes that she needs to develop her pedagogical coaching skills. She feels supported by the structure of the formative evaluation activity, as its design allows her to anticipate student responses, lowering the demands on her.[21] Nicole will gather information about the changes she made, to assess expectations. She wants to collect all student responses to the formative questions. She also wants to ask her students to provide written feedback on the new activities, their usefulness, and how safe students feel to join the discussion.

Nicole's case illustrates how examining one's own practice, while using literature on "good teaching" as a mirror for reflection, can create a tipping point in motivation for expanding one's repertoire. The strength of the course is that the student teacher's GSR provides a starting point for change. Not only does the realization of what they have already achieved motivate student teachers; by learning how new CPs can be incorporated through modular redesign, new CPs also become practically useful (congruent, instrumental, positive cost balance) and hence attainable.

Recent evaluations support this. From the responses of twenty out of fifty students, we can conclude that student teachers highly appreciated making the GSR and reflecting on learning needs and possible changes. One student teacher remarked that evaluating her GSR helped her identify developmental points: "I thought, oh great! I have now captured my routines in one image. The next step is, is this actually OK? So you work rather project-based, so to speak, and at the same time you are allowed to be flexible and check 'What do I actually do?' and 'What suits me? What do I consider important and what is important for my students?'" Student teachers conveyed that their GSR helped them to think about ways to implement new practices. One student teacher explained how he used theory as a reference: "Reading about theory made me think, OK, it is possible to do much more with this, I *want* to do much more with this. That made me change things. So yes, that made me change the image [GSR]." Student teachers also mention that they specifically appreciate the *physical* action of simply moving or (partly) rewriting the Post-its that represent modules (lesson building blocks as well as goals). One student mentioned how the modular redesign activity contributed to her willingness to experiment with new practices: "And then you can start moving them about [*the Post-its*]. That was what I did at least. It really helped me. What can I do with this [*theoretical concept*]? How can I think this through? I do not know whether it [*the change*] is perfect, but it helps you to further experiment. And the fact that you have pasted it out [*with Post-its*] means that you realize what you are going to do; you can easily change again, if it does not work out as you have anticipated."

Not every aspect was evaluated positively. One student teacher stated that making a GSR came somewhat early in her training, as her practice was not sufficiently developed yet, and changed considerably between the start of the course and the redesign assignment. Some student teachers would like more time to discuss their GSR among peers for additional mutual learning. Others indicated that they did not need the discussions about the quality of the scientific articles (a subgoal of the course), as they already learned to interpret such literature in their previous master's degree work. Others found this part to be difficult and considered it not part of the teaching profession.

To conclude, once student teachers have overcome the stagnation in their learning process in the GSR course, they feel more confident to further explore CPs that concern more ambitious forms of teaching.

CONCLUSION

As far as Nicole is concerned, working with a GSR helped her to shape her development as a teacher. Formulating goals that reflected the learning needs she experienced made her willing to change. Professional learning became logical instead of difficult. She experimented with fast feedback activities (as described earlier) and class discussions, supported by her teacher educators and school mentor. Her initial fear of losing control of her students turned out to be unjustified. In fact, the opposite happened. Both she and her students gained more insight in their learning processes, Nicole was able to gear her instructions more to their needs, and students became more engaged. All this had a positive effect on the work atmosphere. Nicole left the teacher education program after a year, with more confidence and more insight into her professional functioning. Her vision of the teaching profession was more developed, and she had found ways to operationalize aspects of her vision and beliefs in her practice. She was aware of developmental points, but she felt equipped to keep learning.

In this chapter, we discussed how we addressed the motivational side of mastering CPs. In essence, we position the need to experience *learning needs* at the center of our practice-based teacher education program. In both courses we have discussed, student teachers were offered top-down references for "what is possible," as much as possible adapted to their situation and concerns, to stimulate reflection on their practice and to support them with examining their learning needs. Such "autonomy support" is needed for student teachers to reflect beyond their own experiences and to be able to make meaningful, knowledgeable decisions about extending their repertoire.[22]

In retrospect, we contend that we further elaborated in our approach the idea of "approximations of practice" by taking a student teacher's perspective.[23] In current PBTE approaches, approximations seem to be designed by teacher educators and researchers.[24] In our approach, student teachers estimate themselves how and when they feel willing and able to master CPs *and* which approximations are suitable for them. Nicole's case showed, for example, how the activity of modular redesign provided her with tools to establish what approximations of formative evaluation and feedback suited her: which adaptations she felt sufficiently confident to make as a first step in mastering this type of practice (a class discussion and the end of her lesson that was prestructured by an FF activity) and which behaviors she identified as important based on the literature and felt she wanted to rehearse (coaching behaviors).

Evaluation of both courses showed that student teachers generally appreciated how the courses were adapted to their learning needs and that deliberate practice and rehearsal became more focused and meaningful to them. Based on these results, and on our experiences both in working with our student teachers and in working with school mentors within our partnerships, we tentatively conclude that we are on the right track. Still, much can be improved, and we face many challenges. We need, for example, to continually pay attention to securing and improving alignment between *all* courses (including, e.g., the subject-specific pedagogy courses). We also are investigating how we can make our one-year program even more adaptive to the individual learning needs of our student teachers. GSRs and modular redesign seem promising ways of realizing this, as these tools allow student teachers to self-assess their teaching practices and personal theories, as a starting point for stepwise development. Finally, alignment with the internships and the quality of the mentoring practices remain a source of concern. We are addressing this issue by developing professional development trajectories for school mentors in cooperation with our partner schools. A current project concerns investigating together with school mentors how GSRs can contribute to mentoring practices in which mentors and student teachers become engaged in co-inquiry. Preliminary results show that GSRs can facilitate deep reflection and can support making connections between practice and theory. We hope that through these initiatives, we all become better equipped to connect theory, vision, and practice and to develop an approach that does justice to the student teachers' knowledge, attitudes, and ideals.

Core Practices That Support Learning to Teach Mathematics Through a Challenging Problem-Solving Approach

Janette Bobis

INTRODUCTION

Current curriculum reform efforts in Australian mathematics education are calling for teaching practices that support the development of higher-order thinking, reasoning, and problem-solving in students.[1] To better prepare elementary preservice teachers to teach in this more socially, intellectually, and emotionally challenging way, I have systematically reshaped the initial teacher education courses I teach to focus on core practices.[2] Such practices include the well-established practices of eliciting, interpreting, and responding to students' mathematical thinking and facilitating whole class discussions. More recently, I have expanded this set of practices to include providing enabling and extending prompts to differentiate student learning.[3] These and other practices are at the heart of an instructional approach that favors inquiry-led and challenging problem-solving tasks.[4] Parallel to these refinements, I have studied and revised my own pedagogies of practice—the strategies and approaches used to develop beginning teachers' understandings and effective enactment of these essential practices.

This chapter has three main aims. First, drawing on research literature and information from preservice teachers' survey responses, lesson plans and post-lesson reflections, I aim to elaborate, explain, and discuss how a research-informed, instructional approach that focuses on challenging mathematics problems is implemented in the broader context of a practice-based initial teacher education program. A second aim is to provide readers with a deeper understanding of the important role core practices play in teaching and learning mathematics through an inquiry-led, problem-solving approach. In so doing, I will address the unfounded but growing criticisms that inquiry-based approaches to teaching mathematics adopted by many initial teacher education programs do not equip beginning teachers with explicit teaching practices needed for the classroom. Finally, the chapter is intended to expand on the existing literature on core practices by elaborating on the use of enabling and extending prompts to support novice teachers in differentiating the learning of students when engaged in challenging problem-solving in mathematics.

THE AUSTRALIAN CONTEXT: PROBLEM-SOLVING, EXPLICIT PRACTICES, AND INITIAL TEACHER EDUCATION

The past two decades have seen a global shift of attention in education toward instruction that promotes conceptual understanding, reasoning, student agency, and inclusion.[5] In mathematics, problem-solving approaches have been considered a major vehicle by which many of these outcomes can be achieved, with curriculum and education policy documents around the world reflecting this view.[6] In Australia, there has been a growing interest in problem-solving approaches incorporating cognitively challenging mathematical tasks to help leverage opportunities to develop these important learner characteristics. Successive versions of the Australian curriculum have emphasized the importance of developing student proficiency in mathematical understanding, reasoning, and problem-solving alongside fluency. However, international comparative tests, such as the Program for International Student Assessment (PISA), indicate that although Australian students perform relatively quite well on mathematics questions requiring recall of facts and procedural fluency, they are not performing as well on the more demanding tasks requiring reasoning and problem-solving.[7] These findings have stimulated renewed recognition of the importance of incorporating challenging tasks into the teaching of mathematics.

Tasks or problems are considered *challenging* when the solution or solution pathways are not familiar to students, and they are required to engage in sustained, deep thinking that will involve effort and persistence. According to Peter Sullivan and colleagues, sustained engagement in higher-order thinking is likely to benefit students' conceptual understanding as well as their fluency because they "are more likely to make sense of mathematics and remember what they have learned if they work on tasks that are appropriately challenging" without being told initially how to solve them.[8] This process of problem-solving prior to instruction implies that learning is inquiry-led and that students' agency grows as they start to view themselves as capable learners who are ready to make autonomous decisions about their own learning.

Of course, preparing students for this type of inquiry-led, problem-solving work involving intellectually challenging tasks requires teaching practices that are "more socially and intellectually ambitious than the current norm."[9] Like that of other conceptually based instructional approaches, the goals of ambitious teaching are founded on the anticipation that *all* learners will develop higher-order thinking, reasoning, and problem-solving skills. Supporting teachers to teach in ways that will achieve these goals requires explicit attention to specific core practices that also need to be integrated into initial teacher preparation courses. Sadly, an erroneous belief exists with some Australian policymakers that inquiry-led problem-solving approaches imply a lack of explicit teaching practices on the part of teachers, and there is a perception that initial teacher education (ITE) programs incorporating such approaches are not adequately preparing our future teachers.[10] A possible reason for this perception is the lack of specificity regarding teaching practices mandated by the Australian Institute for Teaching and School Leadership (AITSL) as part of the standards that ITE programs must meet to be nationally accredited.

The standards are grouped into three domains of teaching: professional knowledge, professional practice, and professional engagement.[11] In reality, teaching practices are relevant to all three domains, but they are most prevalent in the professional practice descriptive statements. Although AITSL claims that the statements make explicit what effective teachers should know and be able to do across four career stages ranging from graduate to lead teachers, the statements are by necessity quite general. For instance, under the domain of professional practice for graduate teachers, section 3 requires graduates to be able to "plan for and implement effective teaching and learning." Seven descriptive statements follow and are intended to elaborate, including Statement 3.2, "Plan, structure and sequence learning programs: Plan lesson sequences using knowledge of student learning and effective teaching strategies," and Statement 3.3, "Use teaching strategies: Include a range of teaching strategies."

As noted in the example descriptive statements, the standards by which ITE providers develop their courses provide little explicit guidance as to what "effective teaching strategies" to include. However, it is implied in AITSL documentation and understood by ITE providers that the teaching strategies incorporated into their courses must be evidence-based as proof of their effectiveness. Unfortunately, ITE programs are not required to specify the nature of the practices they focus on in their publicly available course outlines. The lack of specificity leaves them open to criticism from individuals conducting purely desktop searches of ITE courses.

Unlike US providers, most Australian ITE providers do not overtly incorporate core practices into their teaching outlines, or if they do, the core practices would not be labeled as such because they are not commonly understood by accreditation authorities. Indeed, the term *core practices* is still not familiar to most Australian teachers or teacher educators. However, there is a growing number of Australian educators who design and study practice-based teacher education reforms to deliberately strengthen the evidence base surrounding the practices that support novice teachers as they learn to teach.[12] My own attempts to make the teaching practices embedded in my primary mathematics ITE courses explicit and evidence-based led me to incorporate core practices almost two decades ago. The increased emphasis on inquiry-led and challenging problem-solving approaches in the curriculum recently motivated me to expand the set of core practices to ensure my preservice teachers were properly supported to effectively implement them.

Researchers warn that the enactment of problem-solving approaches in the classroom is complex and can be problematic unless teachers are properly supported. Charalambos Charalambous and colleagues suggest that this complexity is caused by the need for teachers to identify, select, or create optimally challenging tasks in the first instance and then to know not only how to adjust these tasks to suit different students' needs but also how to support all students solving the tasks as they unfold in the lesson while still retaining cognitive demand and student agency.[13] Designing tasks that are optimally challenging for a heterogeneous group of students is difficult—what one student finds challenging, another student will find easy. The belief that *all* students benefit from instructional tasks that are optimally challenging assumes that explicit teaching practices are needed to help teachers provide high-quality inclusive mathematical opportunities for all learners. One aspect of teaching emerging from Australian research for this purpose is the use of enabling and extending prompts to help differentiate mathematics instruction while keeping the level of challenge within each student's optimal level of cognitive demand.[14]

ENABLING AND EXTENDING PROMPTS: CORE PRACTICES FOR INCLUSIVE INSTRUCTION

Enabling prompts are intended to engage students who, after a period of unassisted exploration, are not progressing on the original challenging task. Such enablers might involve a reduction in the number of steps, the use of less complex numbers, or a variation in the representation involved in the task. For example, consider the challenging task intended for students ages five to seven years: *Five students have twenty-one counters between them. Each student has a different number of counters. How many counters might each student have?* A suitable enabling prompt might be to reduce the number of counters or the number of students in the problem. Another enabler might involve the use of concrete materials to model various solutions. Significantly, the enabling prompt is still connected to the main problem-solving task and is likely to support struggling students to reengage with the original task without the teacher telling them how to solve it. On the other hand, extending prompts are used to extend students who find the original task easy and are intended to elicit higher-level thinking involving the abstraction and generalization of solutions for the same problem. For the above example, a suitable extending prompt might require students to explain how they know that they have found all the possible solutions.

Most of the research surrounding how teachers view, design, and use enabling and extending prompts has been conducted with practicing elementary teachers. In a study involving twenty-nine early years teachers participating in a professional learning project focused on sequences of challenging mathematics tasks, James Russo and colleagues found that teachers consider prompts to be an important aspect of their practice when teaching with cognitively challenging tasks and that they used them in a manner consistent with how they were intended.[15] That is, teachers mostly prepared prompts prior to their lessons and generally made the prompts available to students after they had engaged with the main task for some time—ensuring that students accessed enabling prompts only when the original task was beyond their capacity or accessed an extending prompt when a greater level of challenge was appropriate.

The use of enabling and extending prompts can have positive impacts on student learning of challenging mathematics problems. Researchers exploring the impact of variation in the level of support offered to novice problem-solvers from a Canadian university found enabling prompts that gradually fade in the level of assistance resulted in significantly more learning than high levels of assistance or assistance that gradually faded out.[16] Meanwhile, students in grades 3–6 reported that consistently having access to enabling prompts allowed them to take control of, and to be successful in, their learning of mathematics.[17] Although further research exploring the effects of enabling and extending prompts on elementary students' learning of mathematics is still needed to improve our understanding of when and how these prompts work best, evidence indicates that they can help promote student agency and inclusion in learning challenging mathematics.

Several studies have also explored how teachers use enabling and extending prompts. In one study, researchers found that upper elementary teachers used prompts for a range of reasons, including to assist students who were struggling with the core task, to promote student conceptual understanding of the mathematics, to encourage students who lacked confidence, and to generally facilitate more successful experiences for students. Conversely, teachers generally used extending prompts to help maintain the level of cognitive demand, to extend the thinking of particular students, or to encourage them to apply their knowledge.[18] These findings resonate with those of earlier studies indicating that elementary teachers perceived enabling and extending prompts as helpful for differentiating instruction involving challenging problems. For instance, Doug Clarke and colleagues found that using prompts was the most frequently used teaching strategy by experienced upper elementary teachers to encourage student persistence on challenging tasks.[19]

Only a few studies have documented the difficulties teachers experience designing and enacting prompts. For instance, in a study of four early years elementary teachers participating in professional learning involving the design and enactment of enabling/extending prompts, Louise Hodgson reported teacher difficulty designing appropriate prompts, providing in-the-moment support to students, and adjusting preprepared enabling prompts on the fly.[20] Similarly, Charalambous and colleagues examined four experienced elementary teachers as they designed and enacted prompts as part of their involvement in a professional development project. Teacher-perceived challenges when designing and using prompts were reported as well as those noted by the researchers during classroom observations. These challenges included the incorrect use of prompts in terms of the mathematics content and its teaching, procedural use of prompts rather than applying them in appropriate circumstances, inchoate use or overuse of prompts, and impediments caused by contextual difficulties such as insufficient time to preprepare them. Significantly, Charalambous and colleagues noted that their study provided "testimony that teaching ambitiously is not a mission impossible for typical teachers."[21] Their analysis of the difficulties encountered by teachers as they learned to engage with enabling and extending prompts helps deepen our understanding of how to support "typical" teachers learning to enact them.

In short, research indicates that it is possible to differentiate learning utilizing inquiry-led approaches and cognitively demanding problems with the assistance of explicit teaching practices such as enabling and extending prompts. However, it is difficult to design and enact such complex practices, and teachers will need professional support to learn to do so effectively. Arguably, in a classroom intent on high-quality instruction that is intellectually challenging and inclusive, enabling and extending prompts are core practices essential for experienced and novice teachers to learn.

Decomposition of Practice: Enabling and Extending Prompts

A teaching practice can be viewed at various grain sizes. The decomposition of a complex practice involves its breakdown into meaningful components or smaller grain-sized practices and identifying and explaining them. Decomposition can allow discussion and rehearsal of complex practices by teachers who want to learn how to enact them. To better understand how we might support teachers in designing and enacting enabling and extending prompts, it is useful to first decompose the practice.

Previous analyses of practicing teachers' use of enabling and extending prompts have helped identify some important components of the practice.[22] A synthesis of prior research findings suggests that there are at least six key steps or practices involved in enacting enabling/extending prompts that occur at two major stages of mathematics instruction. First, at the lesson planning stage, an appropriately challenging task needs to be selected or created. Second, likely student responses to the task must be anticipated. Third, the teacher can then prepare suitable enabling and extending prompts based on the anticipated student responses. Fourth, during the teaching stage, teachers must remain attentive, ensuring they notice student responses. Fifth, teachers must appropriately interpret these responses and make in-the-moment decisions to select the appropriate prompt for each child. This step is less complex if the student response and corresponding prompt were anticipated during the planning stage. It is more complex if the response was not anticipated and the teacher must respond "on the fly." Appropriately prepared prompts reduce the likelihood of teachers responding to students habitually or with inappropriate responses such as simply telling answers without accompanying instruction that intends to develop student understanding.[23] Finally, an appropriate prompt is provided. The last three steps are likely to occur multiple times in a lesson—for different students and for the same student as they work through a task and meet different challenges.

Decomposing enabling and extending prompts into these six components reveals just how demanding they are for teachers to learn how to effectively use them. Despite this complexity, they are an essential part of developing the expertise of teachers wanting to differentiate instruction so *all* learners can experience intellectually ambitious mathematics teaching. Therefore, it is surprising that I could find no research reporting preservice teachers' experiences of enabling and extending prompts as part of their ITE courses. This gap in the research leaves a huge void in our understanding of how prospective teachers learn to plan and enact these practices and the problems they encounter.

PRESERVICE TEACHERS' ENGAGEMENT WITH ENABLING AND EXTENDING PROMPTS

The aim of my investigation was to explore preservice primary teachers' initial engagement with the core practice of enabling and extending prompts—their perceptions of prompts, how they learned to plan and enact them, and the difficulties they encountered during their engagement. Specifically, I was guided by the research questions: What is the nature of the prompts that preservice teachers (PSTs) plan to support the learning of students? What difficulties do PSTs encounter when designing and enacting enabling and extending prompts? How do PSTs perceive the importance of enabling and extending prompts in their teaching of mathematics?

To address these questions, I examined two lesson plans from each of eight groups of elementary PSTs (twenty-four PSTs and sixteen plans in total) that were jointly planned and co-taught to analyze the nature of the prompts they planned for first-grade students (ages five to seven years). I also surveyed the PSTs ($n=23$) via a five-item online questionnaire following their first attempts to independently plan and enact enabling and extending prompts, and I analyzed post-lesson written reflections ($n=24$) about their practices to gain deeper insights into their own perspectives of enabling and extending prompts. Prior to presentation and discussion of the findings, I provide information about the context and design of the mathematics method course.

Context and Course Design

The development of the elementary mathematics methods course for PSTs in question was conceived from constructivist and situated perspectives of learning. A situated perspective recognizes that knowledge is situated, meaning that some types of knowledge are best constructed in one context rather than another and that the more authentic the context, the more effective the interaction between theory and practice will be.[24] A situated perspective in teacher education acknowledges that settings can be designed to approximate teaching contexts with various levels of authenticity in which specific practices can be rehearsed. This means that knowledge for teaching is situated *in* practice and learned while teaching rather than being taught in one context (university lecture) to be applied in a different future context (school classroom).

The twelve-week semester-long elementary mathematics methods course at the University of Sydney was attended by fifty-four prospective teachers. The course was the first of two such courses in a postgraduate ITE program and occurred prior to any professional field placements. The content of the course focused on the development of children's early number knowledge. In the fifth week of the course, PSTs worked in pairs to conduct individual diagnostic interviews with two first-grade children from a local elementary school. After analyzing student interview responses, three to four PSTs collaborated to plan, rehearse, and teach a sequence of two forty-minute lessons in the final weeks of the course. Hence, the course was designed to assist PSTs not only in learning the knowledge and practices needed to progress children's arithmetical strategies but also in learning *how* to enact the knowledge and practices. The core practices focused on in the course included eliciting and responding to students' mathematical reasoning, orchestrating productive group discussions, using mathematical representations, and teaching toward a clear mathematics instructional goal. As part of learning how to enact each of these core practices, PSTs were introduced to the explicit practice of enabling and extending prompts. For instance, while learning how to respond to students' reasoning, PSTs learned about research-based trajectories of strategy use for early additive and multiplicative thinking and were encouraged to use the trajectories to anticipate and then prepare prompts to support student advancement of strategy use. These prompts included the fading in of supports, such as the use of questioning or a class discussion to help direct student attention to important elements (without telling students), the introduction of various representations (say moving from a diagram to concrete materials to make the problem less abstract), and the gradual reduction in the complexity of the numbers involved. Meanwhile, extending prompts practiced included increasing the complexity of the numbers; challenging students to think of multiple answers or strategies for solving a problem; and asking students to generalize their answers, to pose new problems, or to think and justify instances when their answers would not work (negative knowledge).

PSTs were introduced to and expected to rehearse the practices with their peers during university workshops by embedding them into instructional activities suitable for challenging and advancing the thinking strategies of the young children they interviewed during week five. Rehearsals allowed the PSTs opportunities to trial the instructional activities and the associated new practices within somewhat controlled settings prior to enacting them with a small group of first-grade students, including the students the PSTs had conducted the diagnostic interview with. As part of their preparations for teaching the students, PSTs collaboratively prepared lesson plans. To help scaffold the design and use of enabling and extending prompts, PSTs were provided with a lesson plan template adapted from Elham Kazemi and Allison Hintz that explicitly required the PSTs to anticipate approximately three student responses and prepare at least one appropriate enabling or extending prompt for each type of student response.[25]

During lessons, PSTs collected records of their enactment of the prompts, including still images of children's work samples and short transcripts of exchanges among students or between the teacher and individual students while responding to tasks and prompts. PSTs also made field notes on their lesson plans about which prompt they used and how effective they perceived it to be. The PSTs used these data to stimulate written reflective comments on their enactment of prompts that formed part of the evidence analyzed for this investigation.

Preservice Teachers' Responses

The lesson plans and post-lesson reflective statements were thematically analyzed to identify the information to address the research questions and capture unexpected responses from PSTs as they emerged.[26] For instance, lesson plans revealed the type of student responses PSTs anticipated, the number and nature of the prompts they planned, which prompts were used during the lesson, and their perceived effectiveness. Post-lesson reflective statements also revealed information about the perceived effectiveness of the prompts PSTs enacted and provided insights into their overall views about the importance of prompts and the difficulties they encountered in planning and enacting them.

The items contained in the short online survey required PSTs to rate their overall perception of the importance of prompts and how they used them (e.g., How important do you consider the use of enabling and extending prompts in your teaching of mathematics? 1, not at all, to 4, very important; How effectively do you think you implemented prompts in your lessons? 1, not at all, to 4, very [almost always] effectively). The frequency of responses was calculated and used to help explain PSTs' reflective statements.

The Nature of Prompts Planned by Preservice Teachers   The type and frequency of strategies PSTs used to develop prompts are summarized in table 3.1. Across the eight groups of PSTs and the sixteen lesson plans, twenty-nine enabling prompts were suggested, but only twenty-four of them were considered to satisfy the definition of an enabling prompt discussed with PSTs in tutorials. Five suggestions involved explicitly telling students answers or how to solve a problem without providing any accompanying explanation or attempts to elicit student understanding of the mathematics. The problems PSTs experienced when designing and enacting prompts are elaborated on in the next section, reporting the difficulties PSTs faced. The accepted prompts reflected the breadth of strategies discussed in the methods course; no strategies were employed that had not

TABLE 3.1 *Frequency of strategies used to develop enabling and extending prompts*

	STRATEGY	FREQUENCY
Enabling prompts	Use or vary an existing visual representation to make it less abstract	7
	Connect to prior knowledge or task via questioning	5
	Direct attention to specific features via questioning (e.g., What do you notice here? What's the same? What's different?)	4
	Reduce number or break down the steps in the task	3
	Reduce complexity of numbers or operation	2
	Introduce manipulatives or tool (e.g., calculator)	2
	Slow down instruction by repeating an activity after spotlighting another student's work sample	1
	Use inappropriate enabling prompts	5
Extending prompts	Increase complexity of numbers or the operation	9
	Encourage refinements to and generalizations of solutions	5
	Direct attention to relationships via questioning (e.g., What do you notice here? What's the same? What's different?)	4
	Increase the number of steps	3
	Ask for additional reasoning requirements (e.g., justify or explain how you know you have all the possible answers)	3
	Avoid or remove visual representations to make more abstract	3
	Ask negative knowledge questions (Why can't 65 be an answer?)	2
	Ask students to pose a new task	1

been discussed in tutorials. The two most frequently used strategies for developing enabling prompts were to reduce the abstractness of a problem by using a visual representation and to connect new content to prior learning via teacher questioning (e.g., Have you seen this pattern before? Can you use the information from the task you just completed to help solve this task?)

Lesson plans revealed that all but one group of PSTs exceeded the minimal request for enabling and extending prompts and developed multiple examples for each of their lessons. For example, for their first lesson, Elena, Jon, and Rebecca planned a choral count starting at twenty and required students to count forward by twos. They anticipated that this activity would be very challenging for three students in their group but were unsure of how the fourth student would respond. During the planning phase, three different student responses were anticipated (with corresponding enabling prompts): (1) students can't recognize a pattern in the choral count recording chart (direct student attention by pointing to each column on the chart), (2) students get "stuck" when counting proceeds to larger numbers (use prior knowledge of numbers on chart and discuss similarities in the counting sequence), and (3) students are unable to count backward from numbers off the decade (show preconstructed 100 chart). According to field notes on the lesson plan, the first two anticipated responses eventuated. In both instances, the PSTs enacted the planned enabling prompts and wrote "helpful strategy" in the margin of their lesson plan, which indicates that the prompts had had the desired effects.

One group of PSTs developed only one enabling and one extending prompt for their first lesson but constructed multiple examples for their second lesson after receiving feedback on their plan from their university tutor and after the self-realization during enactment of the lesson that they had not sufficiently planned a response to the full range of students' needs that were likely to arise.

Interestingly, the series of questions used and rehearsed repeatedly in university-based tutorials—What do you notice? What's the same? What's different?—was used as part of both enabling and extending prompts but for slightly different purposes. When used as an enabling prompt, PSTs directed student attention to specific features of a task, such as pointing to a specific row or column of numbers in a choral count recording chart, and then followed with a sequence of questions to encourage identification of patterns. Conversely, when used as an extending prompt, PSTs were typically requiring students to reflect on a range of solutions to a problem to explain their reasoning or to generalize about a major mathematical idea. For instance, Maggie, Joyce, and Phillip asked their group of flexible strategy thinkers whether the similarities and differences they noticed in the place value of digits could help them determine a general strategy for mentally solving other two-digit addition problems.

Difficulties Planning and Enacting Prompts Five instances of enabling prompts planned by three groups of PSTs across their two lessons did not satisfy the definition discussed in the methods course. They involved two types of inappropriate responses. There was one instance of explicitly "telling" students what strategy to use without any follow-up explanation or discussion. For example, Jay, Michael, and Isabel suggested that an enabling prompt for a student struggling with the process of subtracting two one-digit numbers was to "tell student to subtract the smaller number from the larger number."

There were four instances of a second type of inappropriate suggestion used by three different groups of PSTs. This response involved them modeling a solution process but without discussing a rationale for its use with students. For example, in their first lesson involving five students who were emergent counters, Bianca, Andrew, and Josie planned an appropriately challenging task requiring students to orally count forward and backward by ones starting from any number up to thirty in a series of short choral counting activities. Each count sequence was recorded on a whiteboard by one of the PSTs. The lesson plan reveals that PSTs anticipated counting backward when bridging a ten would be problematic for students. They planned an enabling prompt involving three steps: (1) a PST would model the correct count while students were listening and watching the recording, (2) students were encouraged to repeat the count with the other PSTs in unison, and (3) the students were asked to repeat the same count without PST assistance. A more appropriate enabling prompt could have involved directing students' attention to the patterns of digits created by the numbers before or after the point at which they got stuck to help them predict what might come next. The same group of PSTs suggested a similar modeling process for an enabling prompt again in their second lesson, but this time they included an additional suggestion of a visual representation in the form of a previously constructed number chart to prompt students who did not know how to solve the task. The visual prompt was accompanied with questioning aimed at eliciting student thinking about the patterns of numbers in the counting sequence. This additional enabling prompt was considered appropriate because it provided students with an opportunity to autonomously make connections between prior learning and the current task without the PSTs telling them answers without providing an explanation or opportunity for discussion.

Notably, there were no instances of inappropriate extending prompts suggested by PSTs in their lesson plans. Even PSTs who had inappropriately used enabling prompts had no problems planning extending prompts. Although not technically considered a difficulty, the most popular strategy for designing extending prompts was to increase the complexity of the numbers or operations involved in the task. It would be an improvement to PSTs' teaching of mathematics if prompts encouraging higher levels of reasoning and generalization by students were more commonly employed.

Difficulties planning and enacting prompts were also reported by the PSTs via their individual anonymized reflective statements and their responses to the online survey they completed following teaching. PSTs were not explicitly required to reflect on the difficulties surrounding the planning and enactment of prompts per se in their reflective statements, but they were required to comment on *any* difficulties they experienced. Thirteen of the twenty-four statements submitted referred to difficulties either planning or enacting prompts. The most cited difficulty in the planning phase, noted by five PSTs, was that of knowing the "different levels of students" so that the most likely responses could be anticipated and thus allow appropriate prompts to be developed. Although the PSTs had conducted a clinical interview with the first-grade students to assess their early number knowledge only a few weeks prior to teaching them, many PSTs were surprised by how quickly the students had progressed since that assessment. One PST reflected that the lesson plan template assisted her planning and teaching "specifically in anticipating students' responses and planning how we responded with appropriate enabling and extending prompts." She then explained that she expected "with practice, I will learn to know my students better and to start scaffolding back versus starting from what the learners can do unaided and scaffold up." The notion of "scaffolding back" versus "scaffolding up" reflects Jay Jennings and Kasia Muldner's notion of gradually fading in support prompts and indicates the PSTs' desire to maintain the cognitive demand of the tasks throughout the entire problem-solving process.[27] Interestingly, prior research found that practicing teachers working with their own classes also reported difficulties designing appropriate prompts to cater to individual student differences.[28] As suggested by one PST, to design appropriate prompts, it may be necessary—but not sufficient—to know your students well. It may also be important to know a variety of strategies for designing prompts and to practice doing so. In the case of my PSTs, they designed their prompts in collaboration with their co-teachers, were able to rehearse them in tutorials, and received feedback from their tutors prior to enacting the prompts with children. This process of support is not often available to practicing teachers.

Other difficulties noted in prior research with practicing teachers referred to contextual issues and time for planning the prompts. Neither of these difficulties was mentioned by the PSTs. One interpretation of their absence is that PSTs knew that the prepreparation of prompts was an expectation of the methods course. They were also given time and support in tutorials to design them.

Most difficulties reported by PSTs referred to the enactment of enabling prompts and included difficulties such as "holding back from telling," "learning to scaffold back," "providing wait time and not rushing forward," and "being comfortable with student struggle." The most reported problem experienced by PSTs when implementing prompts related to responding to the unexpected, namely knowing "how to respond to unexpected student answers" and responding to "unanticipated higher levels of working." This finding aligns with responses to the survey question: Did you create any enabling or extending prompts "on the spot" (i.e., that you didn't explicitly plan)? Sixteen of the twenty-three PSTs responding to the survey reported developing prompts "on the spot." The reported difficulty surrounding the impromptu creation of prompts during lessons corresponds to previous research findings indicating that even experienced teachers find the creation of prompts in the moment as one of the most challenging aspects of implementing prompts.[29] However, as noted in one PST's reflective statement, the occurrence of unanticipated student responses was the stimulus for her to reflect more deeply on students' understandings or strategies and "revise my lesson plan" for the subsequent lesson. What started as a challenge for the PST—dealing with unexpected student responses—became an opportunity for her to think more deeply about student learning for the future.

Preservice Teachers' Perceptions of Prompts   Information about the perceived importance of planning for and implementing prompts in mathematics lessons was conveyed via PSTs' reflective statements and the online survey. All PSTs rated the use of enabling and extending prompts in their teaching of mathematics as either "very important" or "somewhat important" in their survey responses. Reflective statements revealed a wide range of reasons to explain this overwhelming positive response. Most explanations implied that using prompts enabled PSTs to be more responsive to students' needs by "allowing me to differentiate" instruction, "enabled me to extend *all* students' reasoning" and "to adapt lessons to individual's needs," and helped "ensure all students were engaged" in solving the same challenging task.

Another cluster of reasons for the positive perception of prompts evident from the reflective statements related to improving PSTs' learning about teaching mathematics. Prompts were described as "learnable" and therefore a practice that was considered likely to "improve with time and experience." Prompts were also considered to help "my lesson preparation and professional thinking" about teaching mathematics and "increased my noticing" of student strategies and understandings "for assessment and future planning." Within this cluster of reasons, sixteen PSTs mentioned the importance of anticipating student responses in the lesson planning phase, as illustrated by a comment from one PST:

> Anticipation was a pedagogical strategy that proved to be particularly
> beneficial. It made it much easier to teach dynamically because we were
> ready with the response—an enabling or extending prompt. It kept the

lesson moving at a good pace. It is a strategy I will continue to use in an authentic classroom context where there will be a more diverse range of knowledge and learning needs to cater for simultaneously.

In terms of the effectiveness with which they enacted enabling and extending prompts, ten PSTs rated their implementation as "sometimes effective and sometimes not" in the online survey. Eleven PSTs rated them as "mostly effective," and two rated them as "very or almost always effective"; no PST rated his or her implementation of prompts as "never effective." In her reflective statement, a PST noted that her implementation of prompts was more successful when she began "trusting my students a bit more." She explained that "trusting" meant that she learned to "provide students with space" and hold back "explaining" when students appeared to be struggling or were silent. Providing an appropriate prompt, she found students could "figure out things for themselves," and in doing so, she "saw the satisfaction" on their faces. Positive experiences implementing prompts had the effect of PSTs making personal commitments to include such practices in their future teaching.

CONCLUSION

Education policy documents and curriculum reform efforts in Australia are calling for ambitious teaching approaches that promote conceptual understanding, reasoning, student agency, and inclusion.[30] The past few decades in Australia have seen a surge of interest in inquiry-led problem-solving approaches incorporating cognitively challenging mathematical tasks as part of the realization of these reforms.[31] A major obstacle to these reform efforts, however, has been the need to prepare teachers with new types of teaching practices. Of particular concern to teachers is how to differentiate instruction to ensure *all* students are supported in the problem-solving process and experience appropriate levels of challenge. Contrary to some popular beliefs that inquiry-led problem-solving approaches do not involve explicit teaching practices, I have argued here that in classrooms implementing such approaches, enabling and extending prompts are explicit practices essential for experienced and novice teachers to learn.

I also argued that given the prompts' complexity, it is essential that practicing and preservice teachers are supported as they learn how to effectively implement these prompts. This preparation and support should start in ITE programs—where multifaceted practices can be decomposed for closer study and practiced in authentic educational contexts that are less complex than whole class settings.

Surprisingly, no study to date has focused on understanding preservice teachers' experiences of enabling and extending prompts. This chapter addresses this gap in the research and increases our understanding of how prospective teachers learn to plan and enact these practices and the problems they encounter. Significantly, due to contextual differences for the professional learning of practicing and novice teachers, the problems they face are not identical and therefore need further investigation. The revelation that even novice teachers can successfully learn to design and enact prompts and have positive experiences doing so is proof that all teachers can learn to teach more ambitiously.

CHAPTER 4

Practice What You Teach

Using Core Practices to Improve Connections Between Theory and Practice in Secondary Teacher Preparation

Kirsti Klette, Inga Staal Jenset, and Gøril Brataas

INTRODUCTION AND CONCEPTUALIZATION

Researchers agree globally on the importance of connecting theory and practice in teacher education, and studies have underscored the need to provide teacher candidates with opportunities to practice and rehearse specific teaching methods.[1] Learning about teaching is not the same as learning to put teaching methods into practice—doing the actual work of teachers. Therefore, practical teacher preparation and concrete teaching methods, such as how to organize a classroom discourse, provide feedback, or model solving a specific task, must appear in university courses and not be available only through field placement courses. Accordingly, many university programs are adopting practice-based teacher education (PBTE) and transforming their campus courses to expand preservice teachers' practical experience.

This chapter assesses such a redesign for a five-year integrated university-based teacher education program at the University of Oslo, Norway. Between 2010 and 2012, we redesigned the program to make it more coherent and better aligned with the key practices that prospective teachers should know and be able to perform. Central to our ambition was providing teacher candidates with extensive opportunities to rehearse and learn about core practices relevant for their classroom teaching within a coherent program design.

In this chapter, practice-based teacher education refers to professional preparation that focuses on novice teachers' opportunities in learning how to teach. Curricula in PBTE are often designed specifically to be part of the course content; thus, campus courses employ teaching practices that support understanding everyday classroom teaching.[2] The teaching practices of these curricula have been called core practices, which are, broadly, sets of strategies, routines, and activities that teachers unpack for learning across subject areas, grade levels, and contexts.[3] Incorporating core practices within a curriculum implies rethinking how a teacher education program focuses on ensuring that teacher candidates develop adequate knowledge relevant for classroom teaching.

We begin this chapter by conceptualizing the meaning of core practices and their pedagogies and then outline Norwegian teacher education and the University of Oslo program. We provide a short methodology section before we go on to describe illustrative cases from how we have used core practices in our redesign efforts.

Core Practices

As mentioned, learning about teaching methods is not the same as learning to put methods into practice and using them in complex classroom settings—what Mary Kennedy termed the problem of enactment in teaching.[4] Consequently, several scholars have argued that teacher education programs need to be (re)designed to ensure that candidates learn to think and act as professional teachers in their actual work.[5] This emphasis on practice implies that the curriculum and accompanying assignments and tasks deliberately focus on specific core practices during coursework and do not leave this part of teacher training to the field work and collaborating schools.

Pam Grossman, Karen Hammerness, and Morva McDonald identified six criteria as critical when trying to define core practices—that is, practices that occur with high frequency in teaching, which novices can enact in different classrooms, curricula, and instructional situations and which they can begin to master. These features have provided the basis for common frameworks when trying to develop key characteristics of core practices.[6]

A key aspect when trying to delineate and define core practices is the problem of generic versus specific subject-specific ones. To what extent do the generic practices, such as organizing small group work or providing instructional explanations, need to be tailored to a specific subject or content area? Conversely, are there subject-specific practices—such as modeling argumentation and thinking skills in social science or facilitating text-based instruction for writing a factual text in language arts—that cut across content areas? We believe that this distinction is a false dichotomy; many subject-specific practices are not unique to that subject, and they may have relevance for or transfer to other content areas. For example, there are strong commonalities in argumentation skills in social science, language arts, and science classrooms. Thus, when reporting on our use of core practices in our teacher education program, we provide examples from generic core practices (i.e., how to provide substantial feedback) as well as subject-specific practices (i.e., use of modeling and strategy use and instruction in language arts classrooms).

A related, albeit different, dilemma connected to using core practices as a means of practice-based teacher education is what Dana Grosser-Clarkson and Michael A. Neel termed "predefined enactment approaches" versus "open-ended" ones, underscoring the dilemma of fidelity versus flexibility.[7] Predefined enactment approaches refer to more or less predesigned classroom activities connected to specific subject matter content or instructional activities, such as choral counting in mathematics or oral language assessment in language arts.[8] After the teacher educator has modeled and decomposed the classroom activity, teacher candidates are given the opportunity to rehearse and enact that same activity. Open-ended enactment approaches point to teaching practices that cut across content areas and subjects, such as eliciting students' thinking or orchestrating a class discussion. Within these practices, training does not necessarily involve a common activity or particular content but pays attention to the critical subcomponents of that teaching practice that cut across these activities (e.g., anticipating student thinking and problems when presenting a new content area or ways of strengthening student engagement). While most of the illustrative examples in this chapter refer to teaching situations that might be described as open-ended, following Grosser-Clarkson and Neel's definition, the issue of flexibility versus fidelity is also a key dilemma in these situations.

Pedagogies of Core Practices

To learn a complex core practice, teacher candidates must identify parts and steps that constitute the practice's performance. For this purpose in particular, decomposition, representation, and approximation of the practice are critical steps and strategies for investigation.[9] *Decomposition* of the practice is its segmentation or division into constitutive elements to facilitate teaching and learning. For example, for classroom discourse, this means sub-elements such as posing questions (and tasks) that enable multiple viewpoints and interpretations, involve several students, go on for an extensive period (more than three to five minutes, etc.), or are supported by teacher uptake that calls for clarification or expansion of an idea or by the teacher's way of recapturing or revoicing students' ideas. Thus, when training teacher candidates, teacher educators must develop and use specific vocabulary to refer to each of the practice elements, name its sub-elements, and encourage the candidates to use those terms.[10] *Representations* of practice provide novices with opportunities to see and understand different ways in which a practice is performed in the professional context.[11] Videos, lesson plans, teaching materials (i.e., PowerPoint presentations, handouts), and student work samples can be used as resources.[12]

In the current chapter, we use videos from authentic classrooms and related teaching materials as means of representing practice. The selection of representations depends on the facets of practice that teacher educators want to present. For example, while lesson plans may describe and operationalize *teaching goals* and *intentions* of a classroom discourse fairly well, video representations might be required to represent and decompose the complexity of this specific teaching practices. The selection of representations requires teacher educators to understand the core practices and the content that they want to make visible to the teacher candidates and to provide a common terminology for discussing teaching and learning.[13] *Approximations* of practice refer to opportunities to enact practices in conditions similar to authentic teaching practice. These consist of gradually bringing teacher candidates closer to teaching, targeting specific elements of a discrete practice, creating conditions to reduce complexity, applying new strategies, and limiting the consequences of failure.[14] Such approximations must be structured and include support to help teacher candidates deepen their understanding of the complexity of the core practice at stake.[15] In rehearsals or role-plays, teacher candidates take on and enact the teacher's role. The teacher educator supports and gives feedback to the candidate, with other candidates playing the role of students. These approximations or rehearsals of practice will never replace the need for teacher candidates to engage in actual practice settings; however, the work done in courses can prepare candidates better for practice challenges by instilling ways for them to interpret and understand professional practice.[16] Therefore, it is necessary to offer teacher candidates multiple opportunities to approximate different practices, as these bring the candidates closer to authentic teaching. In addition, research has indicated that candidates profit from using *multiple* sources of representations for the purpose of developing core practices relevant for their prospective classroom setting.[17]

Cycles of Learning Practices As argued, pedagogies of core practice in teacher education involve opportunities to decompose a practice, analyze its representations, and approximate its enactment. Morva McDonald et al. and Kiomi Matsumoto-Royo and María S. Ramírez-Montoya term this "learning cycles" and "cycles of practice," respectively; that is, following a sequence that enables candidates to master teaching in specific areas.[18] Iterative learning cycles are organized to include (1) introduction, (2) preparing and rehearsing, (3) enacting, and (4) analyzing and steps to move forward. Matsumoto and Ramírez-Montoya's review of literature on core practices between 2000 and 2016 pointed to learning cycles of concrete classroom practices as a major area of teaching core practices, while few studies highlighted simulations or collaboration between field and campus courses.[19] Similarly, Marieke Van der Schaaf et al. showed that the content of learning cycles in core practices mostly focuses on classroom learning and aspects of classroom climate and interaction and with less frequency on using pre-lesson and post-lesson activities (e.g., reflective logs and journals, teacher collaborations, and joint discussions) for the purpose of core practice learning cycles.[20]

Core Practices and Program Coherence

Opportunities to enact teaching practices within a coherent program design—that is, the way that different program parts (field placement, foundational courses, methods courses, research methods courses, assignments, and assessment tools) are structured so that they provide a coherent and shared vision—is strongly underscored in the literature.[21] Consequently, program designers must pay attention to how the different components of a program (i.e., clinical and academic components) work together to support candidates' opportunities to experience a consistent and shared vision of what they should know and be able to do. The literature distinguishes analytically between conceptual and structural coherence.[22] *Conceptual coherence* underscores how the elements and components of a program build on a shared understanding among the faculty with regard to the knowledge, skills, and dispositions that teachers must develop, including a shared view of assessment practices and knowledge of the subject matter. Rather than providing a mixed and contrary message, faculty within a coherent program need to share similar ideas and principled thinking regarding the kind of teachers the program will produce, the practices and conceptual language they should use, and the possibility for preservice teachers to do more than reproduce the teaching they experienced in schools.[23] Following Hammerness, programs designed to be more coherent may offer "mutually reinforcing ideas" and "repeated experience with a set of ideas."[24]

Structural coherence, on the other hand, refers to how student opportunities to learn are organizationally and logistically coordinated in order to achieve a common goal. When activities, assignments, and experiences across university and clinical settings align with a program's conceptual vision, the program has "structural coherence."[25] This includes the "logistical organization of coursework" based on a shared vision and the linkage between "courses and clinical experiences. . . . to support, reinforce, and reflect those shared ideas."[26] For practice-based teacher education focusing on core practices, structural and conceptual coherence means that key ideas are evident as building blocks across the program, visible in academic and clinical courses, required reading, and assignments and in individual instructors' work. The sequence of academic courses and arrangements for clinical or field placements in a specific program should be seen as a plan for how conceptual and structural coherence come together to "deliberately build understanding of teaching over time."[27]

While embracing coherence as a critical indicator when redesigning teacher education programs, scholars simultaneously underscore challenges linked to keeping such programs coherent. Thomas H. Levine et al. pointed to academic traditions and faculty autonomy, diverse faculty backgrounds, different theoretical orientations, and limited pressure for change in teacher education as key hindrances for program redesign and coherence.[28] Aligned with this, Levine et al. underscored the role of "pathway flexibility," which is recognizing how conflicts, resistance, and fragmentation are embedded in redesign efforts in academic institutions.[29] Meredith I. Honig and Thomas C. Hatch, and Esther T. Canrinus et al., also underscored coherence as a process of ongoing work rather than "a state to be achieved."[30]

In this chapter, we report on the redesign efforts at the program level as well as pedagogies of practice by using core practices as a way of linking academic and clinical components in teacher education.

Norwegian Teacher Education and the Five-Year Integrated Master's Program at the University of Oslo

At present, there are four main pathways to becoming a general teacher in Norway: two five-year integrated primary and lower secondary master's programs (for levels 1–7 and 5–10); a five-year integrated secondary master's program (for levels 8–13); and a one-year add-on program (for levels 5–13).[31] All programs have a designated national curriculum for teacher education, but common for all programs is that they should be "integrated and relevant for the profession, and research- and practice-based" (i.e., national curriculum for five-year integrated secondary master's program).[32]

Norwegian teacher education has received increased national attention and support over recent decades. Similar to the international context, Norwegian teacher education has been repeatedly criticized for being fragmented and disconnected from practice.[33] However, unlike in many other contexts, in Norway, this critique was followed by national initiatives and an increase of resources allocated to teacher education. This makes the Norwegian context interesting for studying teacher education, as there has been a targeted push for change, innovation, and developments in the sector over the past decade. For instance, starting in 2017, the four main Norwegian teacher education pathways were to be at the master's level, and a new curriculum was implemented for all programs.[34] Further, a graduate school for teacher education research was established to strengthen research in this area.[35] In addition, substantial resources have been invested in funding targeted teacher education research.[36]

Attention has also been paid to the importance of grounding teacher education in practice nationally, not only in terms of the national curriculum but also to emphasize and allocate resources for creating effective partnerships with schools.[37] A center of excellence in teacher education, ProTed (Center for Professional Learning in Teacher Education), was established in 2010.[38]

Against this backdrop, the Department of Teacher Education and School Research (ILS) at the University of Oslo redesigned its teacher education program in 2010. Until 2012, the program's two courses related to training professional teachers (and not subject-specific courses) amounted to a total of 60 European Credit Transfer System (ECTS) points; that is, 30 ECTS points for foundation or general pedagogy and 30 ECTS points for subject didactical courses, or methods of teaching content classes.[39] Few structures enabled alignment across these courses or securing progression throughout the program. The redesign aimed for a more coherent and practice-based program, emphasizing teacher candidates' opportunities to rehearse, practice, and enact core practices relevant for their prospective classroom work through campus and field placement courses. A reform group was established in summer 2010, and in spring 2013, the revised program model was implemented in ILS's five-year program.

DATA AND DATA SOURCES

In this chapter, we report on experiences with the redesign of our teacher education program and how attention to core practices was prevalent in the reform efforts. We focus on our five-year integrated program, which includes about two hundred candidates every year across a combination of thirteen subjects. All candidates prepare to teach at secondary level (grades 8–13) and in two subjects. As mentioned, the reforms began in 2010 and continued to develop. In the present chapter we report on data sampled through different projects from four cohorts of teacher candidates spanning 2018–2022. Data include five annual program evaluation reports, surveys of 177 teacher candidates on their opportunities to study and enact practice, and research data from two small research projects drawing on thirty-seven logs and eleven interviews with teacher candidates. We also collected video observations of the candidates' fieldwork and screen recordings of their mentoring conversations for a small subset of candidates.[40] Drawing on these data, we will share three illustrative examples of how we worked with core practices as a means of aligning coursework and fieldwork in our teacher education program.

The examples illustrate features of core practices on very different levels of grain size. The first example illustrates work on the overall program design, focusing on four thematic areas as building blocks for a coherent program design. The two other examples illustrate our work on pedagogies of teacher education, one of them within a generic course and the other within a methods course in Norwegian language arts. All three examples center on the use of core practices in an open-design enactment approach.[41] When summarizing these redesign efforts, we especially focus on examples (examples 2 and 3) in which video use, combined with the observation instrument Protocol for Language Arts Teaching Observations (PLATO), has served as a part of the teacher education pedagogy. The PLATO protocol summarizes key facets of effective teaching in language arts, based on the research literature. It divides instructional quality into four domains (instructional scaffolding, intellectual demand, representation and use of content, and classroom environment), which are in turn divided into three or four sub-elements. In this chapter, we pay special attention to the instructional scaffolding domain and the modeling, strategy use and instruction, and feedback elements of the protocol, in addition to the classroom discourse element from the intellectual demand domain. We have used the PLATO protocol as a means of decomposing core practices,

supported with representations of the same practices through video examples from authentic classrooms.

CASES TO ILLUSTRATE THE WORK WITH CORE PRACTICES IN OUR PROGRAM DESIGN AND THROUGH PEDAGOGIES FOR TEACHER EDUCATION

A Broad Conception of Core Practices: Program Design Around Four Practical Thematic Areas

For our departmental redesign, we built on the body of research emphasizing the importance of practice-based teacher education to design a
structure that would ground the program more strongly in practice. We
designed it around four building blocks, or thematic areas from the
teaching profession, as a way to build programmatic coherence.[42] These
four intersecting thematic areas were "teaching and learning," "classroom management and relations," "assessment for learning," and "teaching for heterogeneous classrooms."

The themes were seen as a practice-based core framework that all
courses and seminars were supposed to relate to within a specific timeline
to enable a clear thematic focus that would permeate all seminars and
courses (and accompanying assignments and fieldwork) while at the same
time paying attention to progression. The themes were not defined as core
practices, and their grain level was far too broad to be conceptualized as
specific core practices that candidates could study and enact. However, the
themes functioned as a way to broadly define the most important practices that our program would follow, and we used them to create program
coherence in our redesign efforts, similar to the efforts reported by Levine
et al.[43] The themes also functioned as a starting point for further operationalization of what these broader practices might entail.

For instance, within the thematic area of teaching and learning, the
candidates would first receive lectures on classroom discourse and the role
it can play in student learning. They would later participate in seminars
in their foundational courses, where they would role-play different typol-
ogies of classroom talk and rehearse being the teacher, employing distinct
talk moves to progress the conversation.[44] The candidates would also take
part in subject didactical courses, where they would, for instance, study

how classroom discourse could be used in literature discussions in Norwegian language arts. Finally, the curricula for the candidates' fieldwork, corresponding to the different themes, were aligned with the coursework curriculum.

Findings from program evaluations and teacher candidate surveys indicate that the attention to practice is recognized by the teacher candidates, even though there are indications that they have more opportunities to study and enact practices distant from interactions with students (i.e., planning for teaching, analyzing teaching materials, etc.) than practices closer to the students (i.e., analyzing students' learning, practicing and rehearsing teaching). There are also indications that the pandemic and online teaching produced a small decline in such opportunities.[45] The evaluation also recognizes our program's practice-based work in that the candidates in our program perceived that our faculty use examples from practice (cases, video, transcripts, student work, assignments, etc.) more often than those in many other programs in Norway; indeed, 60 percent of our candidates answered that we do so to "a very great / great extent," compared with an average of 40 percent of candidates across institutions giving the same reply.[46]

A Narrower Conception of Core Practices: Representing, Decomposing, and Approximating Specific Practices Within Courses

This broad conception of core practices across four thematic areas was further operationalized in narrower conceptions, as already exemplified with the attention to classroom discourse discussed earlier. Although there was a push toward grounding the program and its coursework in practice, it was left flexible for faculty to relate to the four thematic areas and adapt them to their subject areas and their candidates. Therefore, our faculty were not required to identify core practices to focus on, and those who did had the flexibility to decide for themselves which core practices to focus on (i.e., open-design enactment approach).[47]

In some of this work, our faculty used video as an instructional tool to represent and decompose specific practices, and some also relied on the operationalization of specific practices from observation manuals (e.g., the

PLATO manual). To further illustrate how we have worked with this narrower conception of core practices in our program, we illustrate this with two examples: one from a "clinical week" on campus and the other from Norwegian language arts coursework and fieldwork.

Practical Training on Campus: Representation and Decomposition of Feedback Using Video and the Protocol for Language Arts Teaching Observation There is one week in our program during which the candidates, through a well-designed campus course, are gradually introduced to a secondary class and their teacher. They gain insight through a variety of data sources, such as the teacher's lesson plan and teaching materials comprising PowerPoint slides and handouts, video captured during teaching (including samples of students' work in the form of oral presentations), interviews with the teacher and four selected students, and survey data from the students (the Tripod survey).[48] The range of data sources gives the candidates a holistic view and thorough understanding of the classroom and the teacher's teaching.[49]

The week is framed within a pedagogy of teacher education informed by the body of research on "learning to notice."[50] The idea is to enable candidates to study practical artifacts and representations from school through different tools ranging from those a professional teacher would use in his or her own classroom to those used by researchers, such as systematic observational protocols like the Protocol for Language Arts Teaching Observation. During the course, the candidates receive different kinds of assignments. For instance, they are asked to observe specific video clips of the teacher teaching and identify her strategies for providing feedback to students. After introducing the candidates to a simplified version of the feedback element from the PLATO protocol, they are asked to observe individually and discuss in groups the features of this element that are recognizable in the video. We sometimes ask them also to compare such predesigned and targeted coding to a more open observation and coding of the same video clip.

Our faculty has been teaching this course since 2018, and in logs and interviews, our candidates report that their observations have become more structured during this course, compared with having only the opportunity to observe and analyze teaching during fieldwork periods, and that the specificity and support for what to observe enables the use of a common vocabulary for describing teaching. As such, the candidates argue that the course provides them a more analytical gaze, rather than mere fieldwork observations, and that the course provides them with a "sharper look" at practice. They also connect this to their upcoming work for their master's thesis and see the connections between a systematic inquiry into a specific classroom and actually performing research on classroom teaching.[51]

Across Fieldwork and Coursework: Use of Video and the Protocol for Language Arts Teaching Observation to Represent, Decompose, and Approximate the Sub-elements of Instructional Scaffolding   Another example of one of our program's innovations illustrates how one Norwegian language arts teacher educator has been using video and the Protocol for Language Arts Teaching Observation domain instructional scaffolding (with strategy use and instruction, modeling and the use of models, and feedback elements) across coursework and fieldwork for a sample of candidates. Research internationally and in Norway has indicated that teachers master some aspects of teaching that are important for teaching quality, such as providing emotional and organizational support, but that other aspects of teaching, such as instructional support, are less developed and have room for improvement.[52] Attention to the instructional scaffolding domain was thus timely in our program.

Over one academic year, the teacher educator steadily returned to the practices of instructional scaffolding during coursework and emphasized, across different subjects' didactical content, the importance of scaffolding student learning and making teaching explicit.[53] Videos of experienced teachers were included during the coursework to represent and decompose the specific practices. The teacher educator often used a simplified version of the PLATO protocol in her teaching; at other times, concepts from the course syllabi functioned to support the candidates' observations and discussions, similar to the example given earlier. Seven of the candidates and their four mentors were followed into fieldwork. The teacher educator asked the candidates to record themselves at three points in time when they planned to try out each of the three practices for instructional scaffolding (i.e., modeling, strategy use and instruction, and feedback) and to select and review the video clips of their enactment with their mentors and peers. Two of the four mentors were trained in the three practices and thus shared a common language and vocabulary with the candidates.

Overall findings from annual evaluations indicate that our candidates value the use of videos during campus coursework, compared with many other pedagogies of teacher education, and that they saw this as a way to visualize what the concepts and theories they had learned in university coursework might look like in practice. Looking at findings from the specific case study on the use of video in our program, video data of the candidates' teaching indicate that the candidates had the potential to enact these practices while teaching, and screen recordings of their mentoring conversations also indicate that the candidates were able to discern the practices' appropriateness in the specific situation.[54] For instance, the candidates would see that a situation in which they had modeled how to use a writing strategy would become too detailed and time-consuming for students who already knew the specific strategy fairly well. The candidates would also reflect on pedagogical dilemmas such as developing strategies to support student writing, albeit without restricting the creativity of the students' writing. Further, the findings indicate that the candidates benefited from studying all three practices simultaneously and in parallel and that practicing one of them seemed to transfer and contribute to the enactment of the other practices. For example, not only did having opportunities to study and enact strategy instruction and modeling and the use of models lead to a high repertoire in strategy instruction and the use of models, but the candidates were also able to enact substantial and specific feedback on students' work because they could refer back to the strategies or models they had been using earlier in the lesson with their students. Finally, in interviews, candidates reported that the use of video and the explicit attention to some specific practices enabled them to engage in more focused and in-depth conversations with their mentors and peers about their enactment of the three practices and their in-the-moment decision-making. This was especially highlighted by the candidates who shared a common language surrounding the three practices of instructional scaffolding with their mentors.

CONCLUSION

Through the illustrative examples presented here, we have shared our experiences of using the concept of core practices to redesign our teacher education program in order to make it more coherent and to connect coursework with classroom practice. The cases illustrate extended opportunities to connect theoretical campus coursework with the practical work of teachers and with their fieldwork in schools. Focusing in particular on some key practices (classroom discourse, feedback, modeling, and strategy use and instruction) helps teacher candidates to develop an "analytical gaze" as well as practical routines and skills relevant for those specific practices; this will also spill over and transfer across practices (i.e., between strategy use and instruction *and* feedback).

Research and evaluations of our program indicate that our candidates value this practical approach to teacher education, and that it helps them connect coursework readings and theoretical concepts with actual teaching practices. Further, outcome data from one of our cases also illustrate that a small sample of candidates was indeed able to contextualize these distinct practices to their own classrooms and students during fieldwork.

Furthermore, our cases have illustrated that working systematically with practices of representation, decomposition, and approximation of practice (i.e., applying pedagogies of practice) contributes to a shared vocabulary and language for describing key facets of teaching. This is decisive for enabling candidates (and their mentors) to talk about their professional issues in a specified, targeted, and detailed way. As such, pedagogies of core practices contribute to fostering a common language of teaching among teacher educators, teacher candidates, and their mentors.[55] This equips all three groups with a concrete and detailed vocabulary when discussing key aspects of specific teaching practices, such as challenges in providing students with substantial feedback and how to model solving a specific task for a diverse group of students.

The present push for teacher education in the Norwegian national context, in terms of innovation and changes focusing explicitly on practice, opens up timely opportunities for changes, as illustrated in this chapter. However, alongside this push, there are also challenges facing the further development of the practice-based program in our case. Faculty in teacher education have diverse backgrounds, for instance in terms of academic traditions and theoretical orientations.[56] Some might hold traditional views of university-based teacher education as primarily being a deliverer of theoretical content. Others might be reluctant to focus too narrowly on practice for danger of losing sight of the overall purpose of education.[57] This is probably also the case in our program, and it reminds us to take that into account in our urge to create a practice-based teacher education program, centered around some core practices of teaching. While striving for unity within a teacher education program, Levine et al. emphasize that conflict and fragmentation will be part of the process. Through a case study of a redesign process around core practices to create programmatic coherence, they illustrate the importance of "pathway flexibility" and indicate the need for continuous discussions among faculty and openness to conflicts and choice of slightly divergent pathways.[58] In future work with our program, further attention to conflict and fragmentation may be necessary, and focusing on "pathway flexibility" might ease this endeavor. Further, our program design, and its focus on an open-design enactment approach, might contribute in that respect because it opens up to a more flexible design for all faculty within our program.[59]

CHAPTER 5

Modeling, Explaining, Enacting, and Getting Feedback

How Can the Acquisition of Core Practices in Teacher Education Be Optimally Fostered?

Matthias Nückles and Marc Kleinknecht

INTRODUCTION

During the past two decades, research on teacher education in Europe and the US has undergone a "competence turn" in which the question of how future teachers can develop competencies that allow them to act flexibly and adaptively in the classroom has become a focal point of interest. In German teacher education, fostering teaching performance has primarily been the focus of the second phase of teacher education. To this end, preservice teachers enroll at so-called teacher seminars after a first academic phase at university where they complete a bachelor's and master's program comprising the study of two or even three academic subjects together with their subject didactics, a curriculum in general pedagogy, and at least two teaching internships.[1] In the academic phase, preservice teachers are provided with scientific, mainly theoretical knowledge and case-based illustrations of teaching and learning (e.g., video-based examples of teaching situations during lectures). However, preservice teachers are provided little opportunity for gaining practical experiences in teaching. In contrast, the subsequent practical phase at the teacher seminars focuses on introducing preservice teachers to professional practice by offering them ample opportunity to collect practical teaching experiences and develop teaching competencies. Teacher educators in the teacher seminars support preservice teachers with practice-oriented courses and feedback on their lesson planning and teaching performance.

This dichotomy of a scientific, mainly theoretical first phase of teacher education, followed by a second, mainly practical phase results in a theory-practice gap, with the consequence that the bulk of the scientific knowledge about teaching that preservice teachers acquire in the academic phase largely remains inert and does not fully become integrated with their experiences during the practical phase of teacher education.[2]

The concept of core practices provides a potential solution to this theory-practice gap because it offers a promising starting point for a shift from "a primary focus on the knowledge needed for teaching to an increased focus on teachers' use of that knowledge in practice" already in the first phase of university-based teacher education.[3] To this end, we have established regular courses on "core competencies of teaching" in the secondary teacher education master's program at the University of Freiburg and in the primary and secondary teacher education bachelor's program at the University of Lüneburg. In the master's program courses in Freiburg, preservice teachers are provided with the research-based instructional principles underlying a number of core practices, such as providing instructional explanations, setting learning goals, and providing feedback to students. In the bachelor's program courses in Lüneburg, preservice teachers at the beginning of their studies focus only on two core practices, managing a transition from one learning phase to the next and providing feedback to students in phases of student seatwork. In addition, preservice teachers at both universities get the opportunity to try out the core practices and apply the instructional principles in microteaching settings with other preservice teachers and to receive peer feedback on their performance.

A major strength of the core practices concept is that the concrete and situated demands of teaching come into focus, which is likely a much more fruitful starting point for educating novice teachers than high-level abstractions from educational effectiveness research such as "cognitive activation" or "supportive climate."[4] Both concepts have recently become popular in teacher training and data-driven development of teaching quality in German-speaking countries.

Following Pam Grossman and colleagues, core practices are high-leverage practices that are essential to the teaching profession.[5] Accordingly, core practices typically occur with a high frequency in teaching (e.g., giving explanations, eliciting and responding to students' ideas) and are relevant for different curricula and subjects. Core practices are *not* simple teaching behaviors (such as "post-question wait time") as they have been investigated in early process-product research on teacher effectiveness.[6] Rather, core practices are holistic activities with a certain level of complexity. Despite their complexity, however, proponents of practice-based teacher education claim that novices can master these practices at a basic level early in their teacher studies. Following Morva McDonald et al., core practices should ideally be research-based—that is, educational research can offer evidence-based recommendations of how a specific core practice should be enacted in concrete teaching situations in order to affect student behavior or student learning positively.[7]

In this chapter, we first will introduce "supporting students' self-regulated reading of expository and narrative text" as a domain of practice that comprises several core practices, for which ample empirical research has been conducted in educational psychology. Second, we will compare the most prominent instructional approach to the teaching of core practices with a well-known skill acquisition model from cognitive science and a novel instructional approach from educational psychology with regard to their implications for the teaching of core practices in teacher education.[8] Third, based on this discussion, we will sketch our own experimental research program on the teaching of core practices. Fourth, we will present main tenets from a first intervention study that marks the starting point of our research program.

SUPPORTING STUDENTS' SELF-REGULATED READING OF EXPOSITORY AND NARRATIVE TEXT AS A DOMAIN OF PRACTICE

In our research program, we decided to focus on supporting students' self-regulated reading of expository and narrative text as a domain of practice, because teachers are often confronted with situations where they need to instruct their students in the self-regulated engagement with demanding texts in various subjects. Annemarie Sullivan Palinscar and Ann L. Brown's reading strategy training called "reciprocal teaching" provides an appropriate instructional activity for defining this domain of practice based on empirical findings.[9] Reciprocal teaching is considered the best studied reading strategy training in empirical research on learning and instruction.[10] Barak Rosenshine and Carla Meister's review of research unequivocally shows that reciprocal teaching effectively fosters the reading competence of students at different age levels and with various learning prerequisites.[11]

Furthermore, reciprocal teaching can act as a container for several core practices because central principles of the well-known cognitive apprenticeship model are embedded in this instructional activity (see table 5.1).[12] These principles include, in particular, the provision of metacognitive knowledge about *why*, *how*, and *when* to execute each strategy (so-called metastrategic knowledge); the cognitive modeling of the reading strategies by the teacher; and the adaptive scaffolding and fading out of support by the teacher as the students progress in their strategic competencies.[13] Hence, not only does reciprocal teaching specify powerful reading strategies for students, but the activity also offers novices the opportunity to try out essential core practices such as (1) giving instructional explanations (of the reading strategies), (2) cognitive modeling (of the reading strategies), and (3) scaffolding students' group work adaptively (in applying the reading strategies; see table 5.1).

Accordingly, to introduce learners to the self-regulated reading of expository and narrative text, a teacher first must explain the purpose of the four key reading strategies (formulating questions, providing summaries, clarifying comprehension difficulties, making predictions) as well as how and when during the reading process they should be executed. Second, the teacher should be able to model each of the four strategies in front of the students. Third, the teacher should adaptively support students as they rehearse the strategies independently in small group work (see table 5.1).

TABLE 5.1 *The three core practices contained within the instructional activity "reciprocal teaching"*

Core practices	Instructional explanation of reciprocal teaching.	Cognitive modeling of the four key reading strategies.	Scaffolding students' collaborative execution of reciprocal teaching.
Teacher activities	Introduce the four reading strategies (e.g. formulating questions to the text). Define each strategy and support each definition with an example. Justify the order in which the strategies should be applied. Define students' roles in practicing reciprocal teaching and explain the course of practicing reciprocal teaching.	Model the reading strategies and think aloud concurrently to share your cognitive processes with the students.	Support the "discussion leader" through questions, explanations, or instructions (teacher takes control of students' collaborative learning process). Support the discussion leader by prompting strategy execution, small group dialogue (e.g., turn taking) or aspects of texts' content (students' control of their collaborative learning process is preserved).

Source: Based on Marc Kleinknecht, Imke Broß, Anja Prinz, and Matthias Nückles, "Ich kann Schüler*innen beim Erschließen von Fachtexten anleiten. Ein Training zum Erlernen einer Kernpraktik" [I Can Support Students' Self-Regulated Reading of Scientific Text: A Core Practice Training for Preservice Teachers], *Journal für LehrerInnenbildung* [Swiss Journal of Teacher Education] 22 (2022): 56–67.

HOW TO BEST TEACH CORE PRACTICES TO PRESERVICE TEACHERS: AN INTERDISCIPLINARY DISCUSSION OF APPROACHES FROM NEIGHBORING FIELDS

In deciding how best to teach core practices, we find it useful to compare and contrast the learning cycle of McDonald et al. with other prominent approaches to the acquisition of complex skills from the neighboring fields of cognitive science and educational psychology.[14] This interdisciplinary discussion allows us to derive a number of novel hypotheses regarding the optimal design of core practice learning environments, which we have begun to examine experimentally in a series of intervention studies.

The learning cycle of McDonald et al. has been derived from research on the professional development of teachers in the tradition of situated learning theory.[15] The learning cycle comprises four phases of learning and instruction. In the first phase, a teacher educator introduces a core practice by modeling it himself or herself or by presenting and discussing a video or written case of a teacher enacting the core practice. This introductory phase serves the purpose of helping preservice teachers develop a concrete image of the core practice as it is embedded in teaching situations. The modeling phase is followed by a second phase, in which preservice teachers prepare for and rehearse the core practice collaboratively with peers, which should make it easier for them to enact the core practice. Then, in a third phase, preservice teachers enact the core practice independently with students in the classroom. Finally, in a fourth phase, preservice teachers analyze their teaching with the help of feedback from peers, educators, or both. The central teaching principles of the learning cycle are therefore the modeling of the core practice, the step-by-step approach to authentic practice (approximation of practice), and the reflection on action supported by feedback from peers, experts, or both.

Interestingly, the learning cycle lacks a phase in which the instructional principles on which the core practice is based are explained by an expert. Also, McDonald and colleagues point out that it is possible to start the learning cycle in any of its phases. Both assumptions, the absence of a phase of principle-based explanation by an expert as well as the absence of a specific starting point of the learning cycle, contradict crucial theoretical assumptions of Anderson's adaptive control of thought–rational (ACT-R) theory. ACT-R is a well-known theory in cognitive science that was developed to model the cognitive processes involved in the acquisition of complex intellectual skills. Originally, the scope of ACT-R was largely confined to skill acquisition processes in well-defined algorithmic domains such as mathematics or programming.[16] However, there is no reason why the fundamental processes postulated by ACT-R should not apply to the ill-defined and nonalgorithmic domain of teaching. Hence, we suggest that

ACT-R can be fruitfully used to conceptualize the acquisition of core practices in teaching.

Following ACT-R, the acquisition of a core practice requires the construction of a declarative mental representation of the core practice first. The psychological notion of "declarative representation" means that a preservice teacher first needs to understand the basic instructional principles underlying a core practice, and, at the same time, she or he should be able to recall and verbalize the principles accurately. For example, preservice teachers should understand that Jacob Kounin's famous classroom-management principle of *withitness* does not mean that a teacher should be able to detect 100 percent of the disruptive moves that students enact during a classroom session.[17] Rather than being an observational skill, withitness denotes a teacher's ability to communicate a stance. Accordingly, successful implementation of withitness implies that a teacher can successfully establish the belief in her students that she is willing and able to detect and to prohibit every single disruptive behavior that occurs in the classroom.[18] Helping preservice teachers develop such a principle-based representation of a core practice allows them to understand its deeper theoretical meaning—in particular, what purpose the core practice serves (e.g., communicating a personal stance), and under which situational conditions the core practice should be enacted (e.g., during the prevention of disruptive student behavior).

However, such a principle-based explanation of a core practice is necessarily abstract and makes it difficult for preservice teachers to develop a concrete image of how to enact the core practice in real-life situations. Therefore, concrete examples that demonstrate for a learner how to enact a skill are an indispensable bridge for helping the learner transform the declarative representation of the skill into procedural—that is, applicable—knowledge. The main contention of ACT-R theory is that procedural knowledge is created as a synthesis of the abstract declarative representation of the skill and the concrete, example-based modeling of the skill. Accordingly, illustrative examples that show preservice teachers how the core practice is competently enacted should necessarily follow the abstract principle-based explanation.

Taken together, both the learning cycle and ACT-R concur in the fundamental significance of providing examples (e.g., in vivo modeling, videos, written cases) that model how a complex skill should optimally be enacted in order to allow the learner to develop a concrete procedural representation of the skill. However, unlike the authors of the learning cycle, ACT-R theorists emphasize the significance of constructing a declarative mental representation as the initial phase of the skill acquisition process. Hence, following ACT-R, the process of learning a core practice should start with a focus on understanding the basic instructional principles underlying the core practice. Also, regarding the sequence of phases of the skill acquisition process, the learning cycle leaves more freedom to the teacher educator ("depending on the goals and purposes of the teacher educator, it is possible to start this learning cycle in any of its four quadrants"), whereas ACT-R unequivocally prescribes the sequence: (1) instruct a declarative representation → (2) convert into procedural knowledge with the help of examples → (3) automate and flexibilize the skill through rehearsal.[19]

The primacy of this instructional sequence has recently been challenged by a novel instructional approach from educational psychology— that is, Manu Kapur's productive failure.[20] To date, productive failure is relatively unknown in teacher training. The difference between this approach and ACT-R is that the learning of a complex skill begins with a "naive" problem-solving phase without prior instruction. A principle-based explanation and possibly a modeling of the skill then follows this naive exploratory phase. As learners almost inevitably fail when trying to solve a complex domain-specific problem, such as a complex problem in math or physics, without domain-specific knowledge, Kapur called his approach "productive failure." Productive failure can indeed be regarded as productive because Kapur and others showed in quite a substantial number of studies that the instructional sequence of naive problem-solving followed by instruction proved to be more beneficial to learning than the "classic" ACT-R sequence with instruction of the skill followed by problem-solving (i.e., enacting the skill with the goal to solve a problem).[21] From this research, it can be concluded that productive failure particularly promotes a deep understanding of the skill to be learned. It is assumed that during the naive problem-solving phase, learners are forced—due to their lack of domain-specific knowledge—to draw on their general prior knowledge, which enables them to generate fragmented solutions and, at the same time, become aware of their knowledge gaps. This activation of prior knowledge in combination with the experience of failure prepares learners to process the subsequent instruction in a very effective way.

Productive failure has so far been studied almost exclusively in algorithmic domains (including physics and statistics) with university students and pupils and hardly at all in teacher education. However, similar to ACT-R, we are convinced that applying this innovative idea from educational psychology to the design of core practice learning environments in teacher education can be valuable and lead to novel research questions. Based on productive failure, we assume for the teaching of core practices that an independent, naive enacting of a core practice might be an important initial learning phase. The potential of such a phase of naive enactment can particularly be seen in the possibility that preservice teachers become aware of their "enacted ideas about teaching" through the experience of failure. Their initial frames of reference, which they have developed during their "thirteen-year apprenticeship of observation" in their childhood and youth at school, could be challenged by such an instructional sequence.[22]

Hence, productive failure provides an interesting third perspective on the teaching of core practices besides the learning cycle and ACT-R theory, although a prestructured preparation and rehearsal phase as an approximation of practice, as in the learning cycle, and also the role of instructor feedback have hitherto not been implemented or discussed in this instructional approach.

LEARNING TO ENACT CORE PRACTICES COMPETENTLY: AN EXPERIMENTAL RESEARCH PROGRAM

Our discussion of different instructional approaches and skill acquisition models has highlighted some fundamental theoretical assumptions and questions with regard to the teaching of core practices. First of all, the question of which phases should compose a core practice learning environment has come to the fore (composition question). There is much reason to assume that a modeling phase of the core practice to be learned is an indispensable ingredient or phase of an optimal core practice learning environment. Also, a theoretical explanation of the instructional principles underlying a core practice by an expert teacher should be an important phase of such a learning environment, especially if core practices are instantiated by research-based sets of instructional activities to create authentic episodes of teaching for the purpose of novice learning.[23] Second, the question of sequencing has emerged (sequencing question): Does it matter with which instructional phase a teacher educator starts in teaching a core practice? Should teaching start with a principle-based introduction of the core practice? Or should it start with a naive enactment of the practice as suggested by productive failure? Or, as another promising alternative, should it rather start with a concrete modeling of the practice to prepare preservice teachers for the principle-based instruction afterward? Indeed, recent results from a study by Inga Glogger et al. seem to favor an initial modeling of the skill followed by instruction relative to a productive failure sequence as control condition.[24] Third, in addition to ACT-R and productive failure, Grossman et al. propose the principle of approximation of practice, which is instantiated in the learning cycle as a "preparing for and rehearsing the activity" phase (approximation-of-practice question).[25] Such an approximation-of-practice phase could be realized within settings where preservice teachers prepare for and enact a core practice with peers, ideally under the supervision of a teacher educator. Fourth, McDonald et al. propose an analysis phase, in which preservice teachers analyze their enactment of the core practice with the help of feedback from peers, experts, or both.[26] The role of feedback is also acknowledged in ACT-R, where the flexible applicability of a skill in relation to changing contextual conditions is achieved by means of external feedback. However, although teacher educators regard the role of external feedback as indispensable, its relative contribution to skill acquisition is still an under-researched question, at least in the domain of teacher education. For example, extant empirical research on feedback in teacher education studies has shown that the combination of peer and expert feedback improved preservice teachers' professional vision in analyzing videotaped teaching situations.[27] However, it is an open question how feedback impacts the ability to enact a core practice competently (peer and/or expert feedback question). Is expert feedback more useful than feedback by peers? Or can the process of learning a core practice be fostered best by a combination of peer and expert feedback?

These are the research questions we have recently begun to investigate in a comprehensive research program on core practices that has been established as a collaborative project between the University of Freiburg and the University of Lüneburg.[28] To address these questions, we have scheduled a series of intervention studies, in which we will vary experimentally, for example, which type of phase is realized in teaching a core practice (e.g., principle-based explanation phase, modeling phase, preparing and rehearsing phase, analysis and feedback phase) and the sequence in which different phases follow each other. As outcome measures, besides the ability to notice (i.e., the ability to select teaching scenes and interpret them based on theoretical principles), we will focus on preservice teachers' ability to enact core practices competently. To this end, we have developed a semistandardized role-play in which preservice teachers are asked to perform reciprocal teaching as a research-based instructional activity that comprises the core practices of explaining, modeling, and scaffolding (the execution of reading strategies). The quality with which preservice teachers are able to enact reciprocal teaching in this role-play will be assessed in detail using a coding system that comprises more than twenty-five subcategories. The main categories are depicted in table 5.1.

To date, only a few studies (e.g., Glogger et al.) have examined experimentally research questions related to the teaching of core practices in teacher education.[29] Moreover, the existing studies so far focused mainly on the acquisition of knowledge and analytical skills, such as the ability to notice and interpret teaching, but not on the ability to perform core practices with real students in an authentic teaching situation. In the following section, we will present results of a first experimental intervention study from our research program in which we addressed the question of sequencing: Should the teaching of core practices start with a principle-based explanation of the core practices? Or should it start with a naive enactment of the practices as suggested by productive failure?

STUDYING FIRST OR ENACTING FIRST? AN EXPERIMENTAL INTERVENTION STUDY

In this study, we contrasted experimentally two differently sequenced versions for teaching core practices. We investigated whether core practices can be acquired more effectively if the learning process starts with a naive enactment of the practices followed by a principle-based explanation and a video modeling of the practices, or if it starts with the studying of the principle-based explanation and the video modeling before enacting the practices based on the provided information. Thus, in line with the theoretical discussion regarding the optimal sequence for teaching core practices, our study addressed a particular facet of the above-mentioned *sequencing question*.

Both versions of the learning environment focused on teaching reciprocal teaching as an instructional activity containing the core practices of explaining, modeling, and scaffolding (students' execution of reading strategies). We conducted the study within regular courses on "core competencies of teaching" in the secondary teacher education master's program at the University of Freiburg.[30]

In the explanation-and-modeling-first group ($n=24$), preservice teachers first studied a theoretical explanation of the reciprocal teaching principles, including the four reading strategies and how to guide students in their self-regulated application of these strategies in form of a videotaped PowerPoint presentation (30 minutes). Afterward, the preservice teachers watched a best-practice video of a teacher who introduced reciprocal teaching to students by explaining and modeling the reading strategies and by scaffolding them in their collaborative execution of the strategies (30 minutes). Finally, preservice teachers taught reciprocal teaching to a small group of secondary students (40 minutes). The text that the preservice teachers used to illustrate the reading strategies was a textbook chapter on the effects of smog on the climate in big cities.

In the enacting-first group ($n=21$), preservice teachers were first asked to teach a small group of secondary students how to proceed in reading and interpreting a demanding expository text (40 minutes). Preservice teachers in this group used the same text on the effects of smog on climate as in the explanation-and-modeling-first group to work with their second-ary students. After this phase of naive supporting of students' self-regulated reading, preservice teachers studied the videotaped theoretical explana-tion (30 minutes) followed by the video modeling (30 minutes). In both intervention groups, preservice teachers were randomly assigned to small groups of about four students, between thirteen and fifteen years of age, from a German secondary school.

Besides these two intervention groups, we further implemented a con-trol group of preservice teachers ("conventional seminar group," $n = 52$) who also studied the videotaped explanation on reciprocal teaching (30 minutes) followed by the modeling video (30 minutes). However, whereas the two intervention groups were given the opportunity to teach secondary students (40 minutes), the preservice teachers in the conven-tional seminar group simply discussed their impressions from studying the theoretical explanation and the modeling video in the seminar with peers (40 minutes). Hence, the control group underwent a sequence that is quite typical for German academic teacher education: preservice teachers receive theoretical input on teaching practices, in this case laudably cou-pled with a video modeling. However, then, instead of offering preservice teachers the opportunity to enact the practices with students, the course remains within the traditional culture of intellectual debate. Hence, by contrasting this control group with the two intervention conditions, we were able also to address, at least partly, the *composition question* men-tioned earlier: Does the opportunity of teaching "real" secondary students in the reading of a demanding scientific text (i.e., enacting the core prac-tices of explaining, modeling, and scaffolding reading strategies) have an added value compared to the classic academic learning opportunity of intellectual discussion?

To assess the effectiveness of these different intervention conditions, we developed multiple measures including (1) a paper-and-pencil knowledge test of the main concepts and principles underlying reciprocal teaching, with ten multiple-choice questions; (2) a video-based noticing test that required students to comment on six short staged videos (classroom scenes acted out by pupils and a teacher) to assess the ability to notice (i.e., select teaching events and interpret them based on theoretical principles), with the scenes featuring a teacher and small groups of pupils behaving either appropriately or less appropriately in terms of the theoretical principles of reciprocal teaching ($\alpha = .69$); (3) a brief questionnaire asking preservice teachers to indicate their perceived self-efficacy in supporting students' self-regulated reading (six items, $\alpha = .84$) and the perceived usefulness of reciprocal teaching (three items, $\alpha = .80$); (4) a semistandardized role-play in which three student actors played their roles based on a written script to measure the preservice teachers' performance in enacting reciprocal teaching with students. We randomly assigned preservice teachers to groups of actors. To analyze the role-play data, we used the coding system mentioned earlier based on the three main categories (i.e., core practices) and their indicators, presented in table 5.1. The coding was conducted by trained coders. Intercoder reliabilities were consistently very good ($.84 \leq \kappa \leq .87$).

The results showed that preservice teachers in both the explanation-and-modeling-first group as well as the enacting-first group performed better than the conventional seminar group in the knowledge test (medium effect) and also in the noticing test (small to medium effect; see figure 5.1, left and middle chart). The higher performance in the noticing test was due to the greater ability to generate alternative suggestions for action with regard to the teacher's behavior in the videos. Furthermore, both the explanation-and-modeling-first group and the enacting-first group reported a higher self-efficacy regarding reciprocal teaching than the conventional seminar group did (large effect; see figure 5.1, right chart). At the same time, the two intervention groups did not differ significantly either in the knowledge test, the noticing test, or their perceptions of self-efficacy. Thus, starting with a naive enactment of the core practices followed by a principle-based explanation and modeling was similarly effective as starting with a principle-based explanation and modeling of the core practices followed by an informed enactment with regard to the acquisition of conceptual knowledge and noticing abilities. Additionally, the results suggest the advantage of including opportunities for enactment in core practice learning environments for understanding of the practices and self-efficacy regarding their use.

FIGURE 5.1 *Outcomes in the knowledge test, video-based noticing test, and self-efficacy questionnaire plotted by intervention groups. Statistical significance is provided for the comparison of the two intervention groups with the conventional seminar group (i.e., the control group). Cohen's* d *indicates the effect size, with values <0.5 classified as small effects, values ≥0.5 classified as medium effects, and values >0.8 as large effects.*

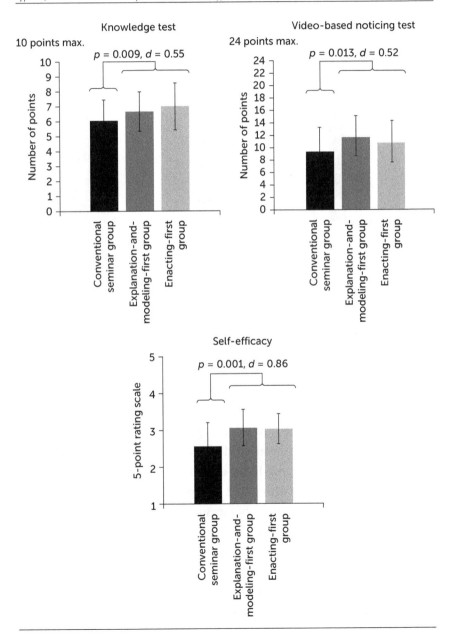

FIGURE 5.2 *Quality ratings of preservice teachers' enactment of the three core practices contained in reciprocal teaching (i.e., explaining reciprocal teaching, modeling the strategies, and scaffolding students' group work adaptively) in the semistandardized role play. Cohen's* d *is the effect size measure, with values <0.5 classified as small effects, values ≥0.5 as medium effects, and values >0.8 as large effects.*

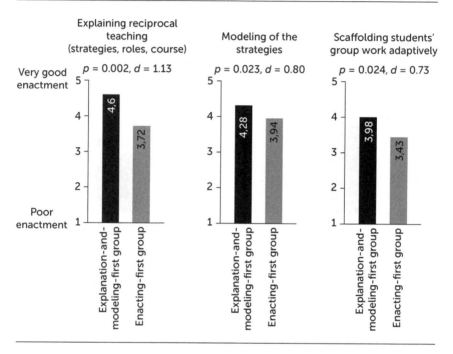

However, the analysis of the role-play data (preservice teachers' performance) of the three core practices (explanation of reciprocal teaching, cognitive modeling of the reading strategies, scaffolding of students' collaborative execution of reciprocal teaching) showed a consistently higher quality of performance in the explanation-and-modeling-first group as compared with the enacting-first group (medium to large effects; see figure 5.2). Apparently, in terms of measured performance in enacting the core practices, a sequence with naive enactment at the start was consistently inferior to informed enactment after the principle-based explanation and modeling of the core practices. However, it is possible that our enacting-first sequence did not work as expected theoretically by the productive failure approach.[31] In fact, our study provides some evidence that preservice teachers who attempted to support secondary students' self-regulated reading naively did not feel that they had failed but, on the contrary, were rather reinforced in their belief that they had competently supported the secondary students in comprehending the expository text. The high ratings of self-efficacy, which were clearly higher in the enacting-first group than in the control seminar group and, at the same time, equally high as in the explanation-and-modeling-first group, support this conclusion.

Furthermore, a detailed analysis of preservice teachers' naive enactments of the core practices shows that preservice teachers without prior instruction about how to teach reading strategies failed to provide instructional support for secondary students on the strategic level. Rather than teaching students strategies for how to approach a demanding text, preservice teachers intuitively acted on the level of text content: most of the time they provided explanations of text content and asked the students questions to make sure that they understood the propositions of the text. This finding suggests that preservice teachers were reproducing the kind of instruction they likely received, in which the teacher's role is to lead the students to the answer, rather than helping students to make sense of the text on their own. Hence, transferring the idea of productive failure to the realm of teacher education needs be more carefully supported, as we did in our initial study reported here.[32] For example, asking preservice teachers to explicitly compare their own enactment of the core practice with the principle-based explanation and modeling example might be a fruitful avenue; such an explicit comparison could make it easier for preservice teachers to become aware of their implicit ideas about teaching, which they have developed during their "thirteen-year apprenticeship of observation," and thereby effectively prepare them for adopting an expert-like enactment of the core practice.[33]

THE POTENTIAL OF AN EXPERIMENTAL RESEARCH PROGRAM ON THE TEACHING OF CORE PRACTICES

In this chapter, we introduced "supporting students' self-regulated reading of expository and narrative text" as a domain of practice that allows preservice teachers to become familiar with a number of core practices, such as providing explanations of strategies, cognitively modeling strategies, and scaffolding students' self-regulated execution of strategies during group work. We proposed Palinscar and Brown's well-known reciprocal teaching as a research-based instructional activity to make these core practices tangible for preservice teachers.

With regard to the teaching of core practices, we contrasted theoretical models from teacher professional development research, cognitive science, and educational psychology. This interdisciplinary discussion spawned a number of research questions that we believe are fundamental to the teaching of core practices: Which phases should a core practice learning environment be composed of? Which sequence of phases supports core practice acquisition best? What is the added value of approximations of practice, such as rehearsing with peers? What benefit results from feedback from peers, experts, or both? We have recently started a research program comprising several experimental intervention studies to answer these questions. The strength of the experimental approach is that hypotheses providing potential answers to our research questions can be tested systematically, and effects emanating from the systematic variation of, for example, a particular phase of the learning environment can be interpreted in a causal sense. Adopting an experimental approach, however, does not preclude that we also conduct thorough qualitative analyses of our preservice teachers' teaching performance and their responses to a video-based noticing test to get a comprehensive picture of their progress in mastering the core practices. Hence, we see our methodology as a mixed-methods approach.

The findings of our first study, summarized earlier, suggest that, irrespective of the concrete sequence position in teaching core practices, enactment of core practices with a small group of students has a significant impact on learning the practices. Similarly, informed enactment after phases of principle-based explanation and video modeling of the principles presumably promotes learning better than naive enactment prior to the explanation and modeling phases. These are, of course, preliminary conclusions that need to be replicated by further studies. Also, our current research program does not address the typically cyclical nature of learning processes, which is of course a limitation.[34] Thus, it cannot be ruled out that the superiority of the explanation-and-modeling-first group over the enacting-first group would decrease if preservice teachers were given the opportunity to go through the sequence of instructional phases once more. On the other hand, it is equally possible that the superiority of the explanation-and-modeling-first group might increase. However, investigating the effects of multiple passes through our core practice learning environments clearly exceeds the scope of our current research project. These are indeed important questions that should be addressed in a follow-up project ideally with a longitudinal study design.

IMPLICATIONS FOR TEACHER EDUCATION IN GERMANY

Reviews of video-based learning in teacher education show that videos are predominantly used to promote preservice teachers' ability to notice—for example, through the critical analysis of their own classroom videos—rather than their ability to act. Since education is still divided into two training periods in Germany, one university-based with higher theoretical components and one at teacher training seminars with more practical components, many teacher educators at universities are likely to see their role as enabling student teachers to critically reflect on teaching based on theoretical approaches and principles rather than enabling them to acquire practical teaching competencies.[35]

In contrast, the rehearsing of teaching, and preparation and reflection, are likely to be seen more as the tasks of lecturers in the teacher seminars and cooperating teachers in schools. Our findings underscore the importance of providing preservice teachers with the opportunity to enact core practices in addition to the phases of principle-based explanation and modeling already present in the university-based stage of teacher education. The findings suggest that a core practice learning environment composed of the phases of principle-based explanation, case-based modeling, and self-guided enactment with "real" pupils in a protected environment can be a very effective learning opportunity in the context of university teacher education promoting preservice teachers' ability to notice and to enact core practices in a professional manner.

CONCLUSION

In our research program on core practices, we will investigate the questions sketched here regarding the optimal composition and sequencing of instructional phases in learning core practices and appropriate approximations of practice, as well as the role of feedback, more deeply in the next few years. Yet, from our reading of the pertinent literature and our own work on core practices, we are convinced that the concept of core practices, as it has been proposed by Grossman et al. and McDonald et al., is indeed a very promising avenue for research on teacher education and, at the same time, a curricular cornerstone around which teacher education and professional development in the twenty-first century should be organized.[36]

CHAPTER 6

Productive Classroom Talk as a Core Practice

Promoting Evidence-Based Practices in Preservice Teacher Education

Alexander Gröschner, Susi Klaß, and Elisa Calcagni

INTRODUCTION

This chapter focuses on facilitating productive classroom talk as a core practice.[1] With regard to teachers' practices of engaging students in classroom talk, empirical research has shown that, across school subjects and grades, teacher-student interaction in the classroom is often dominated by teachers and focused on "correct" and brief student responses. This teacher-led interaction pattern is related to negative effects on student achievement, motivation, and self-concept.[2] Thus, empirical research over the past three decades has begun focusing on evidence-based practices in teacher-student interaction that promote productive classroom talk.

This chapter presents an evidence-based framework for translating and incorporating productive classroom talk into the preservice teacher education program at the Friedrich Schiller University of Jena, Germany, implemented in the Learning-to-Teach Lab: Science (LTL:S). To support this framework, we describe key findings from our research on teacher learning in in-service teacher education. Furthermore, we illustrate how preservice teacher learning about productive classroom talk as a core practice is promoted in practice-related learning environments, such as student teachers' microteaching units and role-play simulations during a teaching practicum. For this purpose, we present a course and ongoing research in the context of classroom-related professional learning opportunities in the LTL:S.

PRODUCTIVE CLASSROOM TALK AS AN EVIDENCE-BASED PRACTICE

Productive classroom talk is a pedagogy that breaks away from interaction patterns that are predominantly steered by the teacher, focusing instead on a classroom culture in which students respect one another and move beyond the boundaries of their own thinking and understanding. Often, productive classroom talk is synonymous with dialogic teaching and educational dialogue.[3] Robin Alexander describes dialogic teaching as follows:

> The need for every teacher to develop a broad repertoire of talk-based pedagogical skills and strategies and to draw on these to expand and refine the talk repertoires and capacities of their students. . . . [The teacher's] responsibility is progressively shared with students, the development and autonomous deployment of whose own talk repertoires is the ultimate goal.[4]

Dialogic teaching, thus, is a framework that can be considered in different instructional approaches of teachers aiming to affect students' ways of thinking and verbal engagement in the classroom. With a strong research background in in-service teacher education, practices of facilitating productive classroom talk have been implemented into preservice teacher education, especially in the US, in the practice-based teacher education movement. In Germany, learning opportunities still need to be included to support planning and the enactment (and rehearsals) of productive classroom talk to generate or expand a talk repertoire of teacher novices.

In the practice-based teacher education movement, high-leverage classroom practices such as leading a discussion and eliciting and interpreting student thinking are promoted in preservice teacher education programs at universities and colleges.[5] In 2008, Pam Grossman and Morva McDonald stated that "university-based teacher educators leave the development of pedagogical skill in the interactive aspects of teaching almost entirely to field experiences, the component of professional education over which we have the least control."[6] Based on John Dewey's idea of laboratory practice, they argued "that research in teacher education needs to return to sustained inquiry about the clinical aspects of practice and how best to develop skilled practice—to add pedagogies of enactment to our existing repertoire of pedagogies of investigation."[7] For this framework, the term *core practices* has been established.[8]

The following criteria have been used to describe core practices:

- Practices that occur with high frequency in teaching
- Practices that novices can enact in classrooms across different curricula or instructional approaches
- Practices that novices can actually begin to master
- Practices that allow novices to learn more about students and teaching
- Practices that preserve the integrity and complexity of teaching
- Practices that are research-based and have the potential to improve student achievement

In line with the criteria, facilitating productive classroom talk is an evidence-based practice that is highly relevant to student learning and motivation.[9] Thus, promoting high-quality verbal teacher-student interaction in the classroom is an important issue that, from our perspective, needs to be addressed at an early stage of professionalization—in preservice teacher education—to increase the frequency of productive classroom talk across subjects, school tracks, curricula, instructional approaches, and so on. Based on a democratic understanding of student participation and student agency for learning, productive classroom talk in teacher-student interaction also contributes to what John Dewey called an embryonic society and "the interaction of mind, [which is] to see how teacher and pupils react upon each other—how mind answers to mind."[10] To address this interaction, we believe that productive classroom talk can be *represented*, *decomposed*, and *approximated to practice* by novice teachers, who have fewer teaching routines in place than experienced teachers.[11] In considering and investigating preservice teachers' learning of productive classroom talk as a core practice, we extend research on dialogic teaching beyond in-service teachers, who have been the main subjects of professional development (PD) intervention studies on productive classroom talk. Before describing our work with preservice teachers, we first review research on productive classroom talk with in-service teachers.

RESEARCH ON PRODUCTIVE CLASSROOM TALK IN IN-SERVICE TEACHER EDUCATION

The activities to promote productive classroom talk outlined in this chapter have mainly been influenced by previous studies on teachers engaged in PD with the aim of fostering dialogic teaching by, for instance, using videos as a tool to reflect on teachers' daily practices. In this section, we report findings from previous research on in-service teacher education and refer primarily to a quasi-experimental study in a metropolitan area in the south of Germany, in which we investigated how teachers participating in a video-based PD program enriched their repertoire for productively engaging students in whole class discussions compared to teachers in a control group (without video-based reflections).

In the past decade, PD programs have been designed to provide teachers with innovative teaching strategies for changing their classroom practices toward a more dialogic teaching style and have been shown to positively affect student learning. According to Nicholas C. Burbules, *dialogic* describes a continuous communication exchange between a teacher and students that, among other things, aims to optimize the initiation-response-evaluation (IRE) pattern toward mutual understanding and greater student contribution.[12] Video-based PD programs such as Accountable Talk, CamTalk, and the Dialogic Video Cycle (DVC) focus on classroom-related interventions and support teachers by offering pedagogical content that has the potential to change everyday teaching.[13] Furthermore, research has shown that teachers' instructional beliefs influence teacher-student interactions. For this reason, PD programs on productive classroom talk have begun to address teachers' beliefs and instructional behaviors in practice—for instance, with teacher reflections stimulated by video examples of their own or another's teaching in PD workshops. These approaches of using video as a stimulus for teacher learning and changing teaching practice through reflection on practice has an impact on research on core practices insofar as video is often used as an artifact providing an accurate replay of the incident that can be reflected on from different angles and by groups with different expertise (peer students, mentor teachers, teacher educators).[14]

As an example, the DVC is a teacher PD program inspired by Hilda Borko and colleagues' Problem-Solving Cycle.[15] The DVC is based on an adaptive design that addresses active learning opportunities in the school context by considering participants' teaching practices via video-embedded conversations about productive classroom talk. The DVC consists of two cycles, each including three workshops and one in-class videotaping of a participant's lesson (twenty-two hours total in one school year). The DVC begins with a briefing, at which the facilitator introduces the program's framework. After that, a workshop addresses lesson planning; teachers bring an existing lesson plan to be revised to incorporate productive classroom talk moves (figure 6.1). The facilitator provides evidence-based talk moves and strategies and encourages teachers to mindfully share and implement talk moves based on their own ideas and experiences.[16] Based

FIGURE 6.1 *The Dialogic Video Cycle.*

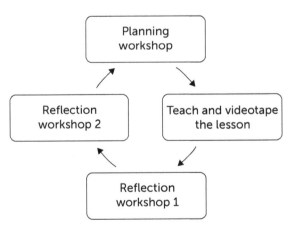

Source: Adapted from Alexander Gröschner et al., "Through the Lens of Teacher Professional Development Components: The 'Dialogic Video Cycle' as an Innovative Program to Foster Classroom Dialogue," *Professional Development in Education* 41, no. 4 (2015): 735.

on their revised lesson plans, the teachers apply the new strategies and talk moves in their classes; these lessons are videotaped. The facilitator then selects short excerpts of the videotaped lessons (about five minutes long) and shares them in two subsequent reflection workshops, using the video material to discuss and reflect on the teachers' dialogic practices in the classroom. In both video reflection workshops, the teachers watch selected video clips, pose questions on productive classroom talk, and jointly reflect on their experiences of verbally engaging in and supporting students' learning processes. Research on the use of video reflection in teacher PD suggests that guiding questions should be provided in this phase—for example, by the facilitator to support and systematize the teachers' thoughts.

Two DVC studies from the 2011–12 and 2016–17 school years produced results central to the objectives of the project regarding teachers, teaching, and students. In total, twenty-nine different subject teachers and their 676 secondary students participated in the study; sixteen teachers participated in the DVC (intervention group) and thirteen teachers in a control group, who attended regular PD workshops on productive classroom talk and ambitious teaching without the use of video as a tool for reflection. In sum, at the end of the yearlong PD program, there were positive changes in teachers' general motivation and satisfaction with the DVC program, in addition to positive effects on teachers' self-efficacy and student-centered beliefs about teaching and learning. No effects on teachers' acquisition of declarative knowledge about productive classroom talk were revealed.[17]

In terms of effects on teaching, pre- and post-test video comparison analyses revealed that DVC teachers more frequently took steps to elicit student thinking through higher-order questioning, asking students to elaborate on their own ideas and offering constructive teacher feedback (see table 6.1).

With regard to students, we identified positive effects on student motivation and subject-related interest, higher-order learning, and student self-efficacy. The evidence-based teaching practices of productive classroom talk were found to encourage teachers to focus on the cognitive, motivational, and situational (social) learning processes of students and, to a

TABLE 6.1 *Teacher talk moves and instructional examples from the DVC*

TALK MOVES	EXAMPLES
Asking students to express their own ideas	"Who else has an idea of how this phenomenon could be described?"
Asking students to elaborate on their own ideas and pressing for reasoning	"Can you explain this in more detail?" "Can you verify this idea?"
Providing constructive feedback and avoiding simple feedback	"This has been a difficult task, and you found a way to connect the two pictures with a creative approach."

certain extent, teachers. Synthesizing these results, table 6.1 shows examples of teacher talk moves that facilitate productive classroom talk derived from the DVC study. These findings are mostly in line with those of other PD programs emphasizing the talk moves of asking students to express their own ideas or reasoning, and challenging student thinking.[18]

With regard to our current work with preservice teachers, we found it particularly helpful that teachers in the DVC focused on very concrete lessons from different subjects (including revising lesson plans under a facilitator's supervision) and specific instructional features of classroom talk for enacting productive teacher-student interaction. Furthermore, short video examples provided in the reflection workshops with the teachers helped them to notice their own and others' behavior (as a component of modeling) and, significantly, to focus on student (dis)engagement. The variety of incidents in the group of teachers was a fruitful base for exchanging teaching alternatives and sharing ideas about talk moves and their enactment in a future lesson.[19]

IMPLEMENTING EVIDENCE-BASED PRACTICES OF PRODUCTIVE TALK IN PRESERVICE TEACHER EDUCATION

In the following section, we describe how we implemented evidence-based practices of productive classroom talk in preservice teacher education. We first provide information about the structure of the teacher education program at the University of Jena, after which we present a course in which talk moves are promoted. The course itself was developed based on previous research in the LTL:S context.

Structure of the Teacher Education Program

At the University of Jena, the teacher education program, which is one of 120 academic programs, comprises five years of study. Jena is the only university in the federal state of Thuringia (one of sixteen federal states in Germany, located in the middle of the country) where secondary teachers are educated (about 17.5 percent of all university students). In general, secondary teachers in Germany (for higher- and lower-track schools) study two school-related subjects that can be combined in different ways (e.g., German language arts / history or geography/sports), along with an equal number of academic courses on content knowledge and pedagogical content knowledge in both subjects (figure 6.2). To become a teacher, students with a general university entrance certificate (*Abitur*) decide on their subjects early and usually make a small number of changes during the teacher education program (for instance, when subject-related requirements are not achieved). From the first day, all students in the teacher education program attend preservice teacher education courses in education sciences as a third academic subject.[20]

Although there is a standards-oriented program of requirements for teacher education in all of the federal states of Germany, the individual teacher education programs do not necessarily share the same content or pedagogical courses, nor do they rely on the same core practices. In the University of Jena's education sciences program, preservice teachers attend similar courses and lectures in the first, second, and third years. Only in the fourth year and for the final term paper and some research-based in-depth courses do preservice teachers select topics from different sub-domains, such as social work and pedagogy, school development, educational psychology, or research on teaching and learning. Interestingly, since the countrywide reform in the early 2000s toward more long-term teaching practice and field experience in preservice teacher education, the University of Jena is the only university in Germany with a six-month teaching practicum in the middle of the study program (in the third year, either the fifth or sixth semester). During this practicum, preservice teachers are

FIGURE 6.2 *Teacher education program at the University of Jena.*

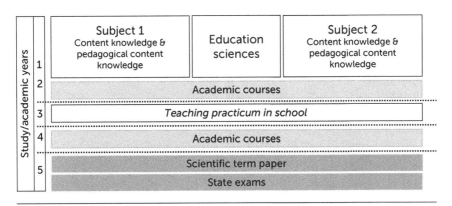

assigned to placement schools (about 250 students per semester in 120 placement schools) across the federal state and beyond. During the teaching practicum, they attend accompanying courses one day every week regarding pedagogical content knowledge related to their chosen subjects or in educational sciences. In this course, all preservice teachers learn about productive classroom talk in theory and practice.

Next, we illustrate how preservice teachers are supported in learning about productive classroom talk as a core practice in the accompanying course of their teaching practicum.

Promoting Productive Classroom Talk in the Learning-to-Teach Lab: Science

In line with the cycle for learning to enact core practices proposed by Morva McDonald and colleagues, productive classroom talk is translated into different activities in the accompanying course of the teaching practicum in the LTL:S (figure 6.3). These activities follow the three steps of representation, decomposition, and approximation of practice.[21]

The course starts with a lecture, in which the preservice teachers are introduced to the concepts of systematic classroom observation (noticing) and dialogic teaching, as well as empirical evidence on teachers, teaching, and students. In addition, some organizational information is presented.

FIGURE 6.3 *Cycle for collectively learning to engage in productive classroom talk.*

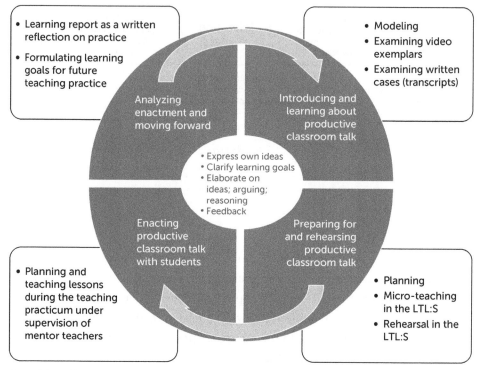

• Learning report as a written reflection on practice

• Formulating learning goals for future teaching practice

• Modeling

• Examining video exemplars

• Examining written cases (transcripts)

Analyzing enactment and moving forward

Introducing and learning about productive classroom talk

• Express own ideas
• Clarify learning goals
• Elaborate on ideas; arguing; reasoning
• Feedback

Enacting productive classroom talk with students

Preparing for and rehearsing productive classroom talk

• Planning and teaching lessons during the teaching practicum under supervision of mentor teachers

• Planning

• Micro-teaching in the LTL:S

• Rehearsal in the LTL:S

Source: Adapted from Morva McDonald, Elham Kazemi, and Sarah Schneider Kavanagh, "Core Practices and Pedagogies of Teacher Education: A Call for a Common Language and Collective Activity," *Journal of Teacher Education* 64, no. 5 (2013): 382.

In the next activity, at another date, videos (mostly video excerpts displaying the talk moves presented in table 6.1) and other materials, such as verbatim transcripts from our previous studies, are used to represent and model productive classroom talk moves.

Preservice teachers are instructed to use a video annotation tool to watch video excerpts (approximately five minutes long) individually and are asked to collaboratively engage in noticing and reasoning about productive classroom talk. The video annotation tool offers the opportunity to stop the video clip, reveal context information (about the class, the lesson, etc.), and add comments to single events or the entire excerpt. The analysis aims to decompose complex teacher-student interactions, which usually get lost during real-time classroom observations without observation training.

With regard to approximating practice, the LTL:S is equipped like a modern classroom (but with more video and audio tools), which allows students to plan, rehearse, enact (teach), and reflect on productive classroom talk moves in whole class discussions and small groups during the accompanying course of the teaching practicum. We provide preservice teachers with a space to experiment with productive classroom talk and reflect on practices through short, simulated role-plays and a microteaching unit (see details below). These opportunities are not guaranteed in placement schools with "real students" and mentor teachers.[22] For this reason, as preservice teachers spend almost six months in the placement schools under the supervision of mentor teachers, the microteaching part of the course aims to encourage them to further transfer and adapt their experiences from the LTL:S to the placement schools through (1) enacting productive talk moves in their own teaching and (2) reflecting on their experiences with the mentor teachers in post-lesson conferences. Thus, the step of approximation has two parts: first, a "safeguarded" training session in the LTL:S and then, subsequently, the adaptation of new knowledge and skills to preservice teachers' classes in the placement schools to learn how secondary students engage in productive talk under real classroom conditions.

Finally, preservice teachers are given an assignment in which they are asked to reflect on the relationship between theory and practice in the simulation/microteaching unit and to provide a learning report that discusses their experiences in the practicum in relation to the research literature and their own assumptions about learning and that formulates learning goals for teaching practices focusing on productive classroom talk.

Next, we describe in more detail the micro-teaching unit on productive classroom talk in the LTL:S.

Studying Productive Classroom Talk in a Microteaching Unit

During the accompanying course of the teaching practicum, preservice teachers approximate the core practice of facilitating productive classroom talk in the LTL:S. As the group of preservice teachers is generally large, students are split into small groups, each attending one microteaching unit during the semester.

Initially developed in the 1970s, microteaching—in which preservice teachers are encouraged to experience evidence-based teaching practices in small groups and reflect on the experiences—is considered an effective learning opportunity. However, in contrast to microteaching as behavioral training for behavior change, we do not aim to practice certain predefined behavioral patterns of verbal teacher-student interaction, but instead use a set of talk moves as evidence-based tools to adaptively shape situations for productive classroom discourse.[23] The microteaching unit lasts about three to four hours and represents an approximation of practice as follows:

1. *Introduction.* At the beginning of the session, the teacher educators (at least two staff members from the Chair of Research on Teaching and Learning co-lead the unit in a team-teaching format) repeat the basic principles of productive classroom talk, referring to evidence from empirical research. The teacher educators are experienced in supporting teachers, student teachers, or both in productive classroom talk. Both teacher educators serve as coaches and facilitators who support preservice teachers during the preparation phase and guide the co-facilitators during the enactment phase (see below). All new junior and senior researchers who join the microteaching unit and serve as coaches and facilitators receive professional training, including knowledge about instructing productive classroom talk and facilitating preservice teachers during the unit, noticing and video observation, and handling technology in the lab (videography, use of the smart board, audio systems, etc.), as well as organization.

2. *Preparation.* The preservice teachers are assigned to small groups (approximately twelve to fifteen novices), and each group receives role-play cards (assigning them the role of teacher, student, or observer/co-facilitator). The "teachers" are tasked with collaboratively planning an introduction to a secondary lesson (math, language arts, or social sciences), which is followed by small group

work. The lessons are supposed to have a practical grounding in real classroom situations and contexts. The "students'" role-play cards include different student participation profiles (i.e., to be silent, talkative, etc.). The "observers/co-facilitators" receive instruction cards with examples of productive talk moves (see table 6.1) and an observation sheet for systematic observation of the "teachers'" performances. This systematic observation should also help them structure the video-based group reflection phase at the end of the unit, which they moderate.

3. *Enactment.* In the subsequent microteaching unit, the task is enacted in the LTL:S and videotaped (seven cameras at each table and a bird's-eye view). During the enactment, the teacher educators and the co-facilitating student teachers support the teacher; they can intervene using in-ear technology without the "students" hearing the interventional prompts. These prompts are productive talk moves derived from research (see above).

4. *Collaborative reflection.* Each teaching unit ends with a debriefing, in which the preservice teachers reflect on their individual roles, their behavior during and engagement in the teaching unit, and their perceptions of the "teacher-student" interaction. They also receive feedback from the "co-facilitators" who observed the performance. The team of teacher educators provides feedback and responds to the preservice teachers' questions. The team also provides further explanations about the talk moves and concrete alternatives for future practices. Table 6.2 illustrates such a reflective discourse during the debriefing.

At the end of each unit, the preservice teachers provide feedback on the course and the microteaching unit. So far, the feedback from preservice teachers has been positive. They generally perceive the opportunity to simulate and reflect on facilitating productive classroom talk practice as relevant and helpful. Even those who were nervous at the beginning of the unit reported being curious about the simulations and having positive associations with their assignment to one of the three roles. Interestingly, preservice teachers who play "students" often refer to specific students with

TABLE 6.2 *Example of the video-based reflection during the debriefing*

Facilitator	"How did you feel when you asked students to express their own ideas and to elaborate on their results more intensively in the plenary discourse after the small-group work?"
Pre-service teacher Lisa (who enacted the teacher's role)	"I felt a bit stressed to ask all students for their own ideas as I don't do this quite often in my classrooms [during the practicum]. Particularly, the one student in the back who was raising her hand very often and started flicking her fingers . . . it was difficult for me to show that I recognized her willingness to respond to the topic because I received the information [from the in-ear instruction] to involve other, especially silent students, too."
Facilitator	[to the group] "What could Lisa do to signal the student in the back of the class that she has seen her, but also clarifying this student that she wants to invite other students, too, to get engaged in the discourse?"
Pre-service teacher Rick (who had the observer's role)	"You could have sent non-verbal signals to show the student that you recognize her and valuable her willingness to say something. Then you could ask someone else and maybe come back to the girl in the back if she wants to add something to this statement or argue if she agrees or not."

Note: The example is based on a facilitators' memory log and our field notes during the second microteaching unit in the winter term 2022–23.

whom they interact in their own classrooms during their practicum as the inspiration for their responses in the role-play. Preservice teachers performing as "teachers" emphasize the valuable and systematic feedback of the group and the co-facilitators and mention wanting to rehearse the unit more often during the teacher education program—for example, for each of their subjects. Preservice teachers serving as "observers/co-facilitators" highlight the challenge of instructing concrete talk moves and being asked to observe the behaviors of "teachers" and "students" at the same time during the unit. The feedback illustrates that preservice teachers are highly motivated, enjoy microteaching, and perceive this learning as relevant for their future careers.

These initial findings correspond with research on approximations of other core practices.[24] In the next few years, we will systematically investigate preservice teachers' learning in quasi-experimental intervention studies. From a teacher educators' perspective, we are optimistic that the combination of these approaches of the learning cycle (modeling, planning, performing, reflecting) in the LTL:S will promote shifts in preservice teachers' knowledge and beliefs about productive classroom talk and productive dispositions for teaching and learning while simultaneously providing opportunities to learn about ambitious teaching practices, such as noticing and enacting productive classroom talk. Evidence from a previous experimental study revealed that preservice teachers benefit, with regard to knowledge acquisition, from facilitating productive classroom talk in video-based noticing and peer-reflection contexts.[25] Future research will build on these findings, as there is still a lack of research on the extent to which preservice teachers' learning can be transferred to classroom practices during the teaching practicum. We aim to contribute to closing this research gap as part of the LTL:S research agenda.

CONCLUSION

This chapter showed how preservice teacher learning about productive classroom talk as a core practice could be promoted in a practice-related learning environment. Drawing on previous research in the field of in-service teacher education, we illustrated how this evidence-based practice has been implemented in preservice teacher education at the University of Jena. Building on the learning cycle of Morva McDonald and colleagues, we focused on selected productive talk moves, which are modeled and practiced in the Learning-to-Teach Lab: Science; video is used as a powerful tool to represent and capture approximations of the practices of productive talk. This cyclical approach to promoting preservice teachers' learning about practices resonates with the initiatives to promote dialogic teaching among in-service teachers that are outlined here. We believe that the tool provides a helpful framework for working with preservice teachers on the topic of productive classroom talk.

We illustrated how the evidence-based practice of facilitating productive classroom talk, as a prominent research field in in-service teacher education, could be translated into preservice teacher education. It should be emphasized that productive classroom talk is situated in practice to promote student learning. This means that not every discussion among students is dialogic, repeatable, or transferable to the same subject in another class in the same school or another course at the same university. Therefore, it is impossible to completely standardize these evidence-based practices of productive talk and approximate this practice to the full extent in a learning-to-teach context. For this reason, our microteaching unit differs from original trainings insofar as it is adaptive to individuals' verbal behavior. Furthermore, initiatives to scale up productive talk moves show that teachers' communicative processes require contextualization (e.g., regarding the lesson, the class composition, the topic, and the tasks) as well as systematization, especially in how to embed and use video examples for reflection. As a consequence, we assume that novices who receive practical learning opportunities at universities and beyond the placement schools will experience productive classroom talk more deeply and reflect on their own experiences as students, their beliefs about teaching and learning, and their methods of encouraging purposeful verbal teacher-student interaction in the classroom in a fruitful way. In this context, the microteaching unit supports the idea of guided experimentation and reflection, even when there is limited time in the program to extensively rehearse productive talk moves. For this, teacher education—at least in Germany—needs more opportunities to combine theory and practice.

Supporting Norwegian Teachers' Collective Learning of Core Practices Through Cycles of Enactment and Investigation

Kjersti Wæge, Janne Fauskanger, and Reidar Mosvold

INTRODUCTION

This chapter explores how a core practice approach can fit into the Norwegian context of teacher education and professional development (PD). Norwegian teacher education is regulated by national curricula and guidelines, and the present curricula favor a practice-based approach.[1] Yet, Norwegian preservice teachers often experience a theory-practice divide in teacher education. Our initial motivation for engaging in a core practice approach was thus to support in-service teachers in developing their ability to use mathematical knowledge in practice.[2] The present curriculum reform calls for "greater professionalization, closer relationships with schools, and research-rich school-based experiences for student teachers."[3] To achieve this, there is a need for PD initiatives that prepare in-service teachers for providing rich practice-based experiences in partnership with teacher education. The present study explores such an approach to PD.

Our study is grounded on the Mastering Ambitious Mathematics (MAM) teaching project, which takes a core practices approach to supporting in-service teachers' development of ambitious mathematics teaching. This approach draws on the Learning in, from and for Practice project.[4] The MAM project involved thirty mathematics teachers from ten Norwegian elementary schools who participated in a two-year professional development initiative that was organized around cycles of enactment and investigation. The cycles involved six phases (figure 7.1):

1. Preparation
2. Collective analysis

FIGURE 7.1 *Cycle of enactment and investigation for professional development.*

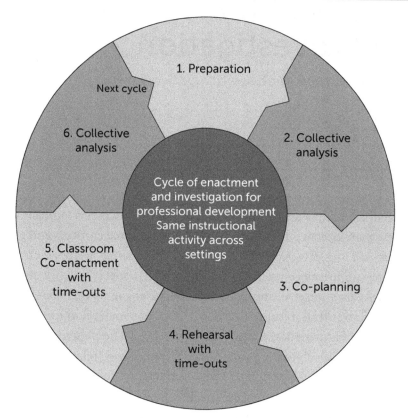

Source: Kjersti Wæge and Janne Fauskanger, "Teacher Time Outs in Rehearsals: In-Service Teachers Learning Ambitious Mathematics Teaching Practices," *Journal of Mathematics Teacher Education* 24 (2021): 563–586, https://doi.org/10.1007/s10857-020-09474-0.

3. Co-planning of instructional activities
4. Rehearsal of instructional activities (without students), with teacher time-outs
5. Co-enactment of instructional activities with students (aged 11–12), with time-outs
6. Collective analysis

Throughout these cycles, our aim was to support teachers in engaging with ambitious mathematics teaching practices. The design of the MAM project resembles Math Labs, where participants develop ambitious teaching through preparing, planning, enacting, and debriefing.[5] Unlike Math Labs, the MAM project also includes rehearsing. In this chapter, we use data from one cycle as a starting point for discussing the potential of using a core practice approach in the Norwegian context. We focus on phases 3–5: co-planning, rehearsal, and co-enactment of a given instructional activity.

Through our investigations, we have found the teacher time-out procedure to be particularly promising.[6] In the rehearsals and co-enactments, the participants could initiate a time-out to discuss something that had arisen. For teachers, time-outs provide opportunities for learning and reflection. We have therefore foregrounded this procedure in this chapter while exploring how the teachers' engagement in co-planning, rehearsals, and co-enactments provides opportunities to work on several core practices of ambitious mathematics teaching.

Our study draws on a conceptualization of ambitious mathematics teaching that highlights student thinking. Among the principles of ambitious teaching are treating students as sense-makers, providing students with equitable access to learning, and seeing teaching as both intellectual work and a craft.[7] These principles involve knowing the students and being responsive to them in culturally appropriate ways. Ambitious teaching is a complex endeavor that places considerable demands on the teacher. As ambitious teaching is grounded in students' emergent ideas, it is crucial for teachers to learn to enact core practices that are responsive to students' in-the-moment thinking. We organized the PD around a set of core practices (hereinafter called practices), including launching problems, using representations, aiming toward a goal, facilitating student talk, and eliciting and responding to students' ideas.[8] Teachers must work on multiple interrelated practices, and the aim here is to explore how a PD initiative can support teachers' engagement with all the interconnected aspects of ambitious mathematics teaching.

TEACHER WORK ON MULTIPLE PRACTICES OF AMBITIOUS MATHEMATICS TEACHING

In the following, we describe how the teacher educator and the teachers worked on the practices of ambitious mathematics teaching in co-planning sessions, rehearsals, and co-enactments. We base our discussion on some illustrative examples with our focus on how these settings provided opportunities for the teachers to share their decision-making and collectively work on multiple interrelated practices and principles of ambitious teaching.

The examples below are from the co-planning, rehearsal, and co-enactment of a quick image activity (figure 7.2). In this activity, students are shown a picture displaying groups of objects for a few seconds. They are then asked to think about how many dots there are and explain how they arrived at the answer.

FIGURE 7.2 *An example of a quick image.*

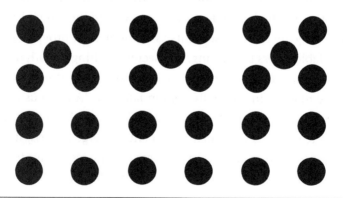

Anticipating Student Thinking and Planning Questions and Questioning Practices

Ambitious teaching is often organized around mathematical discussions that build on students' thinking. Preparation for such mathematical discussions involves engagement in the practice of anticipating student thinking and the careful planning of questions and questioning practices. In this section, we describe how the teacher educator and teachers worked on these practices together in the co-planning phase.

Our analyses show that *anticipating students' mathematical thinking* was frequently discussed across all planning sessions.[9] Our coding indicated that this practice included several dimensions that might be worth further investigation. We also realized that *questioning*, despite being a common practice in teaching, was unevenly discussed across the planning sessions.[10] Like anticipating practice, questioning also appeared to involve several dimensions that might be worth further investigation.

We identified three dimensions of the teachers' anticipating practice from the analysis of the co-planning sessions:[11]

1. *Anticipating students' reasoning*, which involves predicting likely patterns or strategies and using representations.
2. *Anticipating students' understanding*, which includes expectations about students' understanding and what they might be able to do.
3. *Anticipating students' capabilities*, which concerns teachers' views of students' abilities and capabilities.

Similarly, we identified three dimensions of the questioning practice:[12]

1. *Considering which type of question to ask*, often with a focus on guiding students' thinking in a particular direction.
2. *Considering the purpose of questioning*, which often took place in tandem with considering the type of question to ask.
3. *Considering the order and timing of questions.*

In the following, we present and discuss these dimensions using the quick image activity as an illustrative example (see figure 7.2).

Anticipating student thinking is often interpreted as identifying likely patterns, strategies, and student responses. The beginning of this planning session focused on this activity. The teacher educator decided that the teachers should start by exploring and discussing anticipated student strategies before discussing the learning goal for the activity. The planning session thus started with a strong emphasis on anticipating student thinking. The teachers first spent some time writing down expected student strategies individually. The focus was thus initially on *anticipating students' reasoning*, and the teachers focused on predicting likely strategies that students might use in this activity.

The participants also worked on other dimensions of the anticipating practice that go beyond listing likely student responses. The example that follows illustrates how participants considered using or responding to the anticipated student responses. It also illustrates several dimensions of questioning practice. For instance, the example shows several ways that the teachers *considered which type of question to ask. Consideration of the order and timing of questions* was also raised in one of the exchanges.

We join the planning session approximately half an hour into the session, when the following exchange occurred:

1. TE: What should we ask about if this [strategy] is suggested early on?
2. T1: That's what we discussed, how nine can be represented in different ways. It wouldn't be a bad idea to have this one (pointing at another strategy) in addition, and then show that they're almost identical. Perhaps put it underneath the other one.
3. TE: But if they say, "three times nine," yeah, that would have been nice, but the discussion is kind of closed then. So, what kind of question do we ask to move forward?
4. T2: It would have to be a very leading question. "Can you see what she said?" "Nine, what do you think? How do you see nine here?" "Can you identify it in a different way?" And if you then get, "yes, five plus four," then you stop and don't ask any more questions. I think it would be easier for the kids to deal with five and four, and not with the strategy of whoever has a more

challenging way of looking at it, I think. I think it would be easier for them to see the five and the four. I don't think the first thing that would come to their mind is, "Wow, four and four" down there. I don't think that would be the first thing that would come to mind.

5. T1: But if that's what we get, I think it might be smart to ask, "do you see any other patterns?" That we spend some time on . . .

6. T2: . . . To begin with, yeah . . .

7. T1: . . . Yes, to begin with. That we find several patterns.

. . .

This example illustrates how the anticipating practice goes beyond listing likely student responses. For instance, we see here a discussion of how teachers can use the anticipated student strategies to orient students toward a learning goal, how they might respond, and what follow-up questions they might ask. When T2 suggests several follow-up questions that could be asked, this emphasis on questioning is entwined with the focus on anticipating students' reasoning (turn 4). We see here how the teacher educator prompts them directly by asking, "What kind of question do we ask to move forward?" (turn 3). Although it is not made explicit in this situation, we sense that there is an indirect *consideration of the purpose of questioning* involved here as well. When the purpose is to stimulate students to think and consider different strategies, this influences and shapes the questioning practice; considering what question to ask would have been different if the purpose was to check students' understanding of a particular mathematical concept or procedure.

Consideration of the order and timing of questions was raised only in the exchange between T1 and T2. T1's suggestion that asking, "Do you see any other patterns?" might be a good initial question to ask (turn 5) indicates that other and different types of questions might follow. When T2 adds "To begin with" to T1's suggestion (turn 6), this can also be interpreted as an indication of considering order and timing. In other planning sessions, the teachers discussed the order and timing of questions more explicitly.

Elsewhere in the data, we identified situations where the teachers considered *students' understanding* as a dimension of anticipating practice. This is less evident in the present example, but in the last part of the exchange initiated, we do see an indication of how teachers worked on *anticipating student capabilities*:

9. T4: I think different things are involved here. One is to spot it very quickly . . . and then I think the five and the four is the most obvious grouping, because they're used to seeing it on dice, right? And then it's more likely that you'll have more people on board, when you don't extend it too far. Because the longer they're given to struggle with this, the more likely is it that you might hook those who think this is extremely interesting and have a very mathematical mind. And then, along the way, you might have lost those who . . . yeah. So, it depends on where we want to go with this.

10. TE: Yes, and this is kind of what we always need to keep in mind, I think, what we want to emphasize. Yes, T1.

11. T1: When I have done this before, I have shown them [the quick images] quickly twice, like three seconds or so. And then we have gone through some difficult ones too, ones that they don't even get after the two times. But then I have used to, I have had it up there for three seconds, then taken it away, had it up there, taken it away. And those who are very clever will see their pattern and hang on, and then I have left it up there afterward, so the weaker ones are able to spend some more time on it. In that way, everyone has found a pattern, and the clever ones are sitting there with the pattern they saw immediately.

We see how T1 talked about what the "clever" and "weaker" students could be expected to do in this context (turn 11). Such talk about students' capabilities as static abilities can be problematic. When a student is described as someone who *is* weak in mathematics, this can become part of that student's way of talking about himself or herself and can thus delimit the student's opportunities to learn and serve as a self-fulfilling prophesy.[13] Ambitious teaching assumes that all students are capable of ambitious learning. It is thus important to attend carefully to this dimension of anticipating practice.

Exploring Multiple Practices in Time-Outs in the Rehearsals

After co-planning, the participants rehearsed their plans for enacting the instructional activity. In the rehearsals, all members of the group could initiate time-outs, which allow them to think out loud together in the moment of teaching and discuss how the teacher might respond to student ideas and determine the direction in which to take the instruction. We will describe how time-outs in the rehearsals provided opportunities for the teachers to collectively work on practices of ambitious teaching.[14]

Time-outs in the rehearsals focused mostly on the ambitious practices of using representations, aiming toward goals, launching a problem, organizing the board, and facilitating student talk (see table 7.1).[15]

Next, we describe how the participants worked on these practices in the rehearsal, using the quick image activity (figure 7.2) as an illustrative example.

One of the teachers, T4, hereafter called the lead teacher (LT), volunteered to lead the rehearsal while the other participants played the role of students. We present three examples from the rehearsal to show which aspects of the practices the collective sense-making in the time-outs focused

TABLE 7.1 *Frequency of practices per time-out, with percentages for the most frequent practices*

TEACHING PRACTICE	% OF ALL TIME-OUTS IN REHEARSALS ($N = 175$)	% OF ALL TIME-OUTS IN CO-ENACTMENTS ($N = 166$)
Eliciting and responding		39
Using representations	29	21
Aiming toward goals	25	24
Launching a problem	23	
Organizing the board	18	
Facilitating student talk	16	

Source: Kjersti Wæge and Janne Fauskanger, "Supporting In-Service Teachers' Collective Learning of Ambitious Teaching Practices Through Teacher Time Outs," *Scandinavian Journal of Educational Research* 67, no. 4 (2023): 511.

on. In the planning session, the participants decided that the learning goal for the lesson was to learn the distributive property of multiplication—that is, $a \times (b+c) = a \times b + a \times c$. The students in the class knew parentheses from before and had learned the rules about them.

Launching the Problem (Example from Time-Out One)   In most of the rehearsals, the participants worked on the practice of *launching the problem*. One of the aspects they discussed was how the teacher could draw the students' attention toward reasoning and explaining their ideas during the launching phase. This is illustrated in the following example, from the first time-out of the rehearsal.

The rehearsal started with the LT presenting the activity to the other participants, who were acting as students (when we refer to "student" in the rehearsals, we mean the teacher "acting as student"): "I will show you a quick image for three seconds," and then she showed them the quick image. T2 initiated the first time-out of the rehearsal. She looked at the others and asked them: "Are they [the students] first going to say how many they think there are, or isn't that the point?" The LT responded to her question by asking when and how she might ask the students. T2 suggested that the teacher might ask them how many dots there are, stating that "It might not be important, but I just thought there was a logical point to it." The teacher educator then asked the other teachers what they thought about that. T1 proposed that the teacher should draw the students' attention to reasoning and sharing their thinking, instead of focusing on the answer: "I think it's best to just focus on how they're thinking in order to find out how many there are. Not that they are supposed to know that there are twenty-seven. That's not the purpose. It's more about how they have arrived at this." The other teachers agreed, and the LT continued the instruction.

In this example, T2 was uncertain about how the teacher should introduce the problem to the students and wondered whether the teacher should ask the students about the number of dots. This initiated a discussion on how the teacher could orient the students toward explaining and arguing.

Orienting the Students Toward One Another (Example from Time-Out Four)   The practices of *facilitating student talk* and *aiming toward a goal* were also addressed in many of the time-outs. These practices are closely related to each other, and the teachers worked simultaneously on multiple practices. In the example that follows, the participants discuss affordances and constraints from using turn and talk when trying to make room for students' different strategies and *orienting them to each other's ideas and toward the lesson goal*. We join the rehearsal as the lead teacher has represented two student strategies on the board, both by using the quick image and by writing numerical expressions (see figure 7.3). The lead teacher asked whether she should ask for more strategies at this time. The others agreed. T1 suggested that the teacher should ask the students to turn and talk before presenting their strategies on the board. T3 respectfully disagreed and argued that the process would take too long if they did. This initiated a discussion on whether the teacher should use the turn-and-talk approach or not at this point in the lesson. One advantage they pointed out was that all students could share their thinking with each other. A disadvantage, as mentioned by T1, was that the students might copy ideas from each other, which might result in less variation in the student contributions: "But there's the risk that they [the students] might copy what someone else has said and won't offer their own ideas. They might feel that the others have found a way that is quicker and [unclear]. Then we might not get that $5+5+5$ [the sentence at the top of the board in figure 7.3]." T3 suggested that the teacher could use turn and talk when she wanted to highlight connections between strategies: "Perhaps you [teacher] should rather use turn and talk when you have some examples on the board and ask if they [the students] see any connections." The LT agreed and reminded them that in the planning phase they had agreed to use turn and talk to help students focus on the lesson goal.

This example illustrates how the participants worked on multiple interrelated practices. Since the teachers had co-planned the lesson and were learning ambitious mathematics teaching, stopping during instruction enabled them to discuss and share their reasoning about teacher decision-making and multiple practices in relation to principles of ambitious teaching.

FIGURE 7.3 *Student strategies for finding the number of dots in a quick image.*

Making Connections Between Student Strategies (Example from Time-Out Seven)   In many of the time-outs, the participants worked simultaneously on the practices of *drawing the students' attention to the learning goal* and *representing students' ideas* and making connections between different kinds of representations. The participants often discussed which strategies the teacher might select and how to connect different strategies so they could focus on key mathematical ideas. The participants also discussed how the teacher might *represent the students' ideas* to help them see the connection between the different strategies. This is illustrated in the example below from the last time-out of the rehearsal, where the lead teacher represented different student strategies on the board (see figure 7.4). Note the two strategies: $3 \times 5 + 3 \times 4$ and 3×9. We join the rehearsal as the LT represented the student strategy "three times ten minus one" on the board: $3 \times 10 - 1$. The teacher educator initiated a time-out and said that the idea of using parentheses was interesting, referring to the expression $3 \times 10 - 1$ on the board. T5 then marked the representation 3×9 as

FIGURE 7.4 *Student strategies represented on the board.*

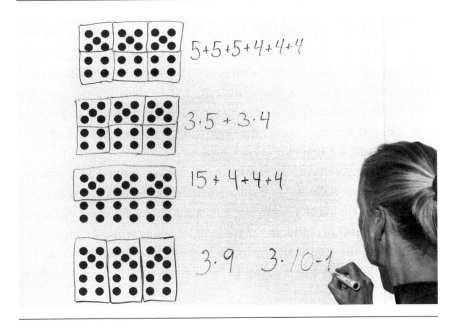

something to address, suggesting they use 3×9 as a starting point to show that $3 \times (5+4) = 3 \times 5 + 3 \times 4$ and thus highlight the distributive property: "I was just thinking the same thing. I was thinking that this [the expression] with 3×9 [on the board] is an excellent opportunity to get them [the students] to see $3 \times (5+4)$. You [teacher] can ask them, 'Does anyone see 9 in another way?' Then we have 5 and 4, and then you [teacher] write down $3 \times (5+4)$."

The LT agreed. T1 suggested placing the expression $3 \times 10 - 1$ below the expression 3×9 on the board to help the students see the connection. The participants then investigated the expression $3 \times 10 - 1$. T2 suggested that the teacher could use parentheses—that is $3 \times (10-1)$—to make a mathematically correct representation of the student's idea, and then ask the students, "Why do you think I put parentheses here?" The other participants agreed, and then they decided where to place the expressions on the board. Next, T5 proposed that the teacher should identify the 4 and the 5 on the quick image, representing 3×9 by drawing circles around them to help the students see the connection: "And you could have drawn it $[3 \times (5+4)]$ too. On the [quick image with illustration of 3×9], the 4 and 5 together, like you did before. Most likely few students see 4 plus 5 in the parentheses. That's maybe difficult." The LT asked how she might do that. This initiated a discussion on how they could represent $3 \times (5+4)$ on the quick image. They decided to first circle the five and the four separately, followed by circling the 5 and the 4 together using a different color (see Figure 7.5).

This example illustrates how the participants considered the practices of *aiming toward a learning goal* and *representing students' mathematical ideas*. We see how the participants' sense-making uncovered the pedagogical dilemma of how to represent the students' thinking while simultaneously considering the mathematical correctness of the representation. This time-out illustrates the complexity of teaching in response to students'

FIGURE 7.5 *Representing $5+4=9$.*

thinking and how the teacher's decision-making involves several ambitious practices simultaneously.

Working on Multiple Practices in the Time-Outs in the Co-enactments

Following the rehearsal, the participants co-enacted the quick image activity with a group of students. As in the rehearsals, the participants could initiate time-outs. In co-enactments, the time-outs focused predominantly on the practices of *eliciting and responding*, *aiming toward goals*, and *use of representations*. Next, we describe how the co-enactments provided opportunities for the teachers to work on ambitious practices.

The students were positioned in a semicircle facing the teacher. The participants sat behind the students so they could listen to and notice their thinking. This was the second time the participants visited this classroom.

Representing Student Ideas (Example from Time-Out One)   The practice of *using representations* is closely related to other ambitious practices, and many time-outs in the co-enactments addressed this practice. As in the rehearsals, we identified situations where the teachers wrestled with the dilemma of how to represent the students' ideas as accurately as possible while simultaneously considering the mathematical correctness of the representations.[16] The following example illustrates this.

The lead teacher began the lesson by launching the problem. She presented the activity and showed the students the quick image for a few seconds. She asked how many dots there were and gave them time to think. The students used the thumbs-up sign when they were ready to share their thoughts. Student 1 (S1) shared: "I first saw that it was 5 on the upper row and 4 on the lower one, and when we got to see it again, I saw that it was three of the two." The LT repeated this strategy as she circled the 5 and the 4s on the quick image on the board. She checked this with S1, "You saw that . . . ?" The LT then asked the students how she could write this by using numbers. Another student, S2, suggested they could write 4×3 and 5×3. The LT initiated a time-out in the instruction. She asked the other participants whether she should write exactly what S2 said or change the order of the numbers (to align with the convention):

LT: In other words, when she said 4×3 and 5×3. Should I have turned them around? Do you see what I mean?

TE: Yes, we see what you mean. What did she say first? If we take that as our starting point?

LT: She said three 5s and three 4s [points at the quick image].

T2: I think it's possible to write the opposite, and then ask if it's the same.

The LT then wrote 5×3 on the board, and asked, "Like this?" The other participants said yes. After she had written the expression $5 \times 3 + 4 \times 3$ on the board, the LT asked the students: "Is this the same as what S1 said?" and continued the instruction.

In this example, the participants considered whether the teacher should focus on the convention relating to the order of factors when representing the students' thinking. Initiating a time-out in the instruction allowed the participants to reason through this dilemma in the moment of teaching.

Supporting Students in Making Connections (Example from Time-Out Three)   The participants also worked on *making connections between different representations* and *considering questions* to ask the students to *orient them toward the learning goal*. These closely related practices were addressed simultaneously in many of the time-outs in the co-enactments. This is illustrated in the example that follows. In the previous rehearsal, the participants had discussed how to use the quick images to support the students in connecting the different strategies. The following example shows how one of the teachers built on this and suggested they ask the students to use the quick image to explain the connection between two answers.

We join the co-enactments as the LT had represented four different strategies on the board. She pointed out two of the expressions, $5 \times 3 + 4 \times 3$ and $(5 + 4) \times 3$ (marked in figure 7.6), and prompted the class to consider whether they could see any connections between them. She then asked the students to turn and talk with their partner. The LT then invited students to share their thoughts. The first two students to share explained as follows: "They're the same numbers, and on the upper row it's 3 twice,

FIGURE 7.6 *Four different strategies represented on the board.*

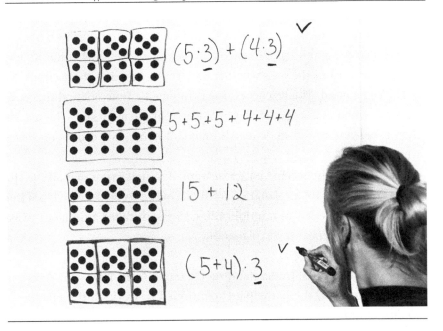

while on the lower row the 3 is only once." The LT marked the number 3 in the two expressions by drawing a line under the 3s. The two students continued with their explanation: "Because the upper one is 5×3 plus 4×3 and the lower one is $5 + 4$ times 3." The teacher initiated a time-out. The teacher educator suggested asking the class: "How do I know it'll be right? How do I know it'll be the same answer?" T2 proposed that they should ask the students if they could use the quick image. The teacher educator turned to the students and asked: "Can the [quick] images be used to explain why, why we get the same answer in the two expressions? [Directs the question at the students.] They can discuss with the students next to them." The LT then let the students discuss in pairs for a few minutes.

Orienting Students to Each Other's Thinking (Example from Time-Out Four)   The next time-out involves the practices of *orienting the students toward the lesson goal* and *orienting the students to each other's thinking*. This example illustrates how the participants considered using specific talk moves to highlight key mathematical ideas. We join the co-enactment as S3, the first student to share after students talked to their partners, explained, "I'm not sure, but on the upper one it's 5×3 and 4×3, while on the lower one, we have added the 5 and the 4 [inaudible]." The LT repeated what the student had said and asked the class whether they could see other connections. No one raised a hand. The teacher educator initiated a time-out and suggested they ask whether another student could repeat what S3 said. The teacher then asked one of the students who raised a hand: "S4, could you repeat what S3 said?"

We see how the teacher educator wanted to make sure that all the students understood the explanation from one of the students, which pointed to the distributive law of multiplication, so she initiated a time-out to ask the students to repeat the explanation.

Supporting Students' Understanding (Example from Time-Out Five)   In the fifth time-out, the participants continued to work on the practice of *aiming toward the goal* and considered how they could use different kinds of representations to support students' understanding of key ideas. We join the co-enactment as S4 responded and repeated in his own words what S3 had said. The LT stopped the instruction and asked what to do next. T1 suggested they look for a new connection, but T5 worried that some students had not seen the first connection yet. He suggested they use the quick images to support the students in seeing the connection between the two strategies, as they had discussed in the previous rehearsal: "So maybe use the figures now, maybe use the green marks on the figures to help them see the connection?" The group agreed.

In this example, the participants recognized that the students were wrestling with understanding the connection between the two expressions, and one of the teachers suggested they use the quick images, as a different representation of the students' ideas, to *support the students' understanding* of the two expressions, as they had talked about in the previous rehearsal.

Aiming Toward the Goal (Example from Time-Out Six)   The last time-out in the co-enactment involved the practices of *orienting the students toward the lesson goal* and *facilitating student talk*. We join the co-enactment as the

LT segued from the previous time-out by elaborating on the students' explanations and pointing out the properties of the distributive property of multiplication (without naming it), using the quick images and the numerical expressions. Next, she asked the students whether they had any questions. The teacher educator initiated a time-out and suggested that she could ask the students to turn and talk to their partner: "See if they can explain the connection to their partner, using the quick images?" The LT then let the students discuss in pairs, and after this, she called the class back together.

This example illustrates the participants' work on *orienting the students toward each other's ideas* and *highlighting the lesson goal*. The teacher educator wanted to engage the students to think and share ideas, and she suggested to ask the students to turn and talk so they could share ideas with each other with a focus on the goal of the lesson.

The remainder of the class discussion centered on the students sharing their ideas on the connection between $5 \times 3 + 4 \times 3$ and $(5 + 4) \times 3$. In bringing the classroom visit to a close, the teacher thanked the students for sharing their ideas, and they smiled and applauded.

LOOKING ACROSS AND AHEAD

Researchers argue that more research is needed to understand how PD can help teachers understand how every aspect of practice is interconnected.[17] In this chapter, we have explored how co-planning, rehearsals, and co-enactments provide opportunities for teachers to simultaneously work on multiple practices of ambitious mathematics teaching. Next, we discuss four perspectives that we consider to be important.

Complex and Multidimensional Practices

Our analysis of the co-planning phase and teachers' collective work on *questioning* and *anticipating* illustrates that these are complex practices that involve multiple dimensions. For instance, *questioning* is not only about figuring out which question to ask, and *anticipating* is not only about predicting a list of likely student responses. Each of these dimensions requires special content knowledge and experience, where attention is focused on the students as individuals and people (and not only on their mathematical ideas). Moreover, we identified some potential constraints in developing ambitious mathematics teaching. Proper execution of the questioning and anticipating practices hinges on the underlying principle of considering students as sense-makers. If this underlying principle is ignored, questioning and anticipating practices might develop in a direction that is contrary to ambitious mathematics teaching. For instance, more than a century of classroom research on questioning indicates that classrooms are dominated by teacher questioning, and the traditional pattern of communication in classrooms is that the teacher asks a question, the students respond, and the teacher provides an evaluation of the response.[18] Decades of classroom reforms have struggled to break this pattern. When teachers prepare for lessons by predicting likely (or desired) student responses, there is a danger that their listening to students' contributions becomes primarily evaluative and confirmatory.[19] We propose that a restrictive noticing or listening practice can be avoided by challenging the practice of anticipating students' capabilities. Disrupting the common practice of anticipating student capabilities as static and fixed abilities, and instead attending to students' dynamic capabilities, might enable a productive development toward ambitious mathematics teaching practices. In contrast, failing to attend to students' identity and position in questioning practices and failing to consider students' capabilities as dynamic and evolving might undermine the development of ambitious mathematics teaching.

Sharing Decision-Making and Working on Responsive Teaching

Our study shows that the opportunity to initiate time-outs in rehearsals and co-enactments enabled teachers to share their decision-making and collectively work on multiple interrelated practices of ambitious mathematics teaching. The teachers tried out different practices, gave each other feedback, and discussed what the teacher could do in a particular situation, drawing on the principles of ambitious teaching. Being responsive to students' mathematical thinking and using their emergent ideas to orient the students toward the lesson goal is one of the most complex and challenging parts of ambitious mathematics teaching.[20] The time-outs in the two settings supported the teachers' learning of how to respond to students' ideas in the moment of teaching and the development of a shared understanding of ambitious teaching that enabled them to use the principles and practices adaptively in new situations.[21]

Exploring Multiple Practices of Ambitious Teaching

Our study shows how the time-outs provided opportunities for the teachers to explore and make sense of multiple ambitious practices simultaneously and to see them in relation to each other.[22] Thus, the rehearsals and co-enactments supported the teachers' understandings of the different practices as interconnected and not separate aspects of teaching.[23] If we look at the two settings together, the time-outs focused predominantly on the following practices: eliciting and responding, using representations; aiming toward goals; launching problems; organizing the board; and facilitating student talk. However, even though many of the practices are closely related to each other, there were some differences relating to which practices were the most frequent in the two settings. For example, eliciting and responding constituted the most frequent practice in the time-outs in the co-enactments, while it was not among the most salient practices in rehearsals. Thus, the two settings supported the teachers' engagement in complementary aspects of the practices of ambitious mathematics teaching. These findings indicate that both rehearsals and co-enactments are needed for PD to provide teachers with opportunities to learn ambitious mathematics practices.[24]

Complementary Ways of Working on the Practices in Rehearsals and Co-enactments

Our analyses of time-outs in the rehearsals and co-enactments show that there were some differences in *how* the participants shared decision-making in the two settings. Rich collective discussions about possible teacher strategies and moves characterized the time-outs in the rehearsals. The participants asked questions, provided feedback, and thus discussed which decisions to make and why—for example, how the teacher could *make connections between student strategies* and why.[25] Because the participants had the shared experience of the co-planning and the rehearsal and because students were present in the co-enactments, the time-outs in the co-enactments complemented the time-outs in the rehearsals by supplying specific suggestions in shorter exchanges about what the teacher might say or do in a particular situation. Thus, the time-outs in the two settings supported teachers' learning in complementary ways.[26]

CONCLUSION

Development toward ambitious mathematics teaching involves deliberate efforts to work on principles and practices that are complex, multidimensional, and challenging. The approach of the MAM project appears promising in this respect, but implementation of a core practice approach brings both opportunities and challenges.

The core practice approach responds to the emphasis that national curricula and guidelines for teacher education in Norway place on practice-based approaches to teacher education and PD. Several institutions are already implementing learning cycles of enactment and investigation from the MAM design in their teacher education programs, and the experiences so far are promising. Preservice teachers and in-service teachers appreciate the closer connection between content and methods, and this approach opens up new ways of collaborating between teacher educators at universities and teachers in schools. At the same time, a restructuring of university courses in this way is also challenging. Facilitating learning cycles in close collaboration between universities and schools requires resources, time, and energy. This can be particularly challenging for teacher educators who lack experience with this kind of practice-based approach to teacher education. The latter challenge is, however, already being addressed, as a national course for mathematics teacher educators has been implemented that involves multiple experiences with MAM cycles and emphasizes literature on core practice approaches to teacher education.

CHAPTER 8

Future Directions for the Field

Urban Fraefel and Pam Grossman

What is commonly referred to as *practice-based teacher education* is expanding into a movement that spans several continents. The contributions in this volume demonstrate that across a number of countries, many teacher education institutions are increasingly striving to think about how to organize the education of future teachers to better prepare them for classroom practice. Across the field, there is a growing awareness that knowledge about teaching and schools, however extensive, is not sufficient to prepare capable teachers. Nor is it enough to hope that the necessary routines and practical skills will be acquired in internships and practica, especially if the aim is to prepare teachers to enact more ambitious and equitable forms of instruction.

The goal of practice-based teacher education, from our perspective, is to connect more strongly knowledge about teaching, goals for students, and the practices necessary to help students succeed. Learning to enact ambitious instruction in today's often very complex and challenging professional contexts must be balanced with deep knowledge about teaching, learning, and schooling. To ensure that knowledge acquired in professional education does not remain tacit and thus disconnected from the actual work of teachers, more and more universities consider it their task to introduce student teachers to professional practices that are based in research on teaching, learning, and interaction. As far as possible, these universities want to ensure that future teachers have the basic capacities to successfully meet the challenges of the teaching profession from the very beginning of their careers.

One of the goals of those who focus on helping new teachers develop a repertoire of core practices is to provide them with the tools they need to be successful with a wide range of learners. The intent is that teachers will continue to grow their repertoire over time and adapt these practices to the specific contexts in which they find themselves and for the particular students in their classes. Teaching well requires a high degree of adaptivity. For a long time, the prevailing view has been that the ability to teach adaptively and responsively emerges only after extended experience in the profession. We are now witnessing a change of mindset in many teacher education programs, as more teacher educators believe that professional preparation may very well contribute to equipping student teachers with the ability to respond professionally and flexibly to ensure the well-being and learning of their students.

WHAT IS NEW IN THE CORE PRACTICE APPROACH?

A focus on practice is not new in teacher education; there have been many prior efforts to bring teacher education closer to practice. There are multiple examples from the past in which teacher education has tried to bring practice into the university classroom and student teachers closer to practice. As noted in chapter 1, in the German-speaking world, these considerations led to Hans Aebli's concept of the "basic forms of teaching," which has clear affinities with core practices. Other examples might include the popularity of microteaching in the 1970s, which provides opportunities for novices to practice specific skills and teaching techniques. Many teacher education programs have extended the time students spend in classrooms, to provide them with more opportunities to observe teaching in internships and practicum settings. What these approaches usually have in common is that they tend to focus on discrete teaching techniques and observations of more typical forms of classroom instruction.

One thing that distinguishes the core practices approach from earlier iterations is its emphasis on more complex practices, such as facilitating classroom discussion, that encompass a number of distinct components and on developing the ability to adapt a practice for specific learners. As evidenced in the chapters in this volume, scholars have taken up the importance of integrating theory, knowledge, and purposes for teaching with opportunities to learn practices that instantiate these more ambitious instructional goals. Learning to support students in ambitious learning in mathematics or to create more equitable classroom environments requires more than theoretical knowledge. Contrary to a common paradigm that teacher education imparts knowledge to be applied in practice, scholars in the area of core practices take as their starting point that the ability to act flexibly and appropriately is developed in the context of practice itself.

The emphasis on supporting ambitious forms of learning is another feature of the work on core practices that seems to resonate with many scholars. The goal of teaching to support ambitious and equitable learning is built into much of the research on teaching core practices in teacher education, and the complexity of this work has required teacher educators to grapple with how best to support novices in attaining these goals. The authors in this volume focus on practices such as facilitating productive classroom discourse, scaffolding student learning, and reciprocal teaching, all of which represent complex forms of practice.[1]

Given what we know from research on instruction, the likelihood of being able to observe such ambitious teaching practices enacted at high levels in classrooms with diverse groups of students is low.[2] This makes the value of creating both opportunities to see high-quality representations of practice and to try out these practices in the university setting more salient. If teacher education were aimed at sustaining current practice in schools, learning from extended student teaching would represent a strong alternative approach. However, to the extent that teacher educators aim to transform classroom practice, the apprenticeship model in a more typical classroom may not suffice. This may help explain the interest in bringing approximations of practice, including rehearsals and modified forms of microteaching, into the university setting. As the authors in this volume demonstrate, student teachers can learn to describe, analyze, and rehearse ambitious forms of classroom practice in multiple learning cycles. The hope is that they are then better prepared to enact these practices in school settings.

One of the key features of the work on core practices has to do with the granularity with which practice is described. Unlike the techniques described in books such as *Teaching Like a Champion,* which focus on narrow skills and teacher behaviors, largely aimed at classroom management, core practices aim at a medium level of granularity; they are neither about small-step routines on the micro level, nor about rather general domains of teaching, but rather target comprehensible and manageable components of practice.[3] The focus on this medium grain size is primarily pedagogical, but parsing practice in sensible ways for the purposes of teaching and learning is rarely easy.

Core practices have been defined as both general and subject-specific in nature. There are certainly practices, such as facilitating classroom discussion, that cut across grade levels and subject matter, although the specific details of the practice may vary by grade and content. Other practices are inherently subject-specific, such as selecting and launching a mathematical problem or supporting students' historical thinking. We see this range of core practices reflected in this volume as well. Some scholars take as their starting point challenges of teaching and learning in a specific subject, particularly in mathematics, while others focus on more general practices.[4] Although it seems clear that some core practices relate to a specific subject and others are generic in nature and are part of the basic repertoire of any teacher, scholars are still puzzling over the transferability of certain core practices across subject matters or contexts.

There are clear practical implications for how teacher educators design and teach what are traditionally known as "methods classes" in the US or "fachdidaktik" in German-speaking countries and how to design opportunities to learn both more general and more specific core practices across the teacher education curriculum. As noted earlier, there is also a question in the field about whether to target more general practices that cut across content areas, particularly in elementary education, or to focus on the practices that have been shown to be most effective within particular subject matter. This is just one of the questions that remains unsettled in the emerging research on core practices.

EMERGING QUESTIONS AND DIRECTIONS FOR FUTURE WORK ON CORE PRACTICES

A look across the work happening in different national contexts reveals a number of questions that scholars are currently grappling with in the area of core practices. These include definitional work concerning what "counts" as a core practice and how to connect historical work on practices such as facilitating productive classroom talk with emerging work that describes this as a core practice. A second area concerns questions about how best to teach core practices in the context of teacher education, including how best to sequence the activities of representation, decomposition, and approximation; how to create authentic opportunities to try out practice in university classrooms; and how best to develop curricula that support coherence in learning to teach. Another open question has to do with the extent to which specifications of core practices constrain improvisation and adaptation; as Kirsti Klette and her colleagues ask in chapter 4, is the goal of approximations of practice enactments that follow closely the initial specifications of practice, or is the goal more open-ended and flexible approaches to enactment?

Refining Interpretations of the Concept of Core Practices

Repeatedly in recent years, there have been struggles about how to define core practices and at what level of abstraction or concreteness they should be defined.[5] A consensus seems to be gradually emerging that the definition of what constitutes a core practice is informed by a pragmatic perspective—that is, guided by the question of how to identify manageable, comprehensible, and purposeful units of instruction on which teachers must be able to draw in their professional activities and that can be taught in ways that respect the complexity of teaching. Nevertheless, different views remain about to what extent a particular component is a core practice in its own right, an element of it (i.e., a smaller unit), or even a higher-level domain that can encompass multiple core practices. For example, even in editing this volume, we have debated whether approaches such as dialogic teaching or reciprocal teaching represent core practices, in their own right, or instructional activities that might include multiple core practices, including facilitating productive classroom talk and eliciting student thinking. In recent work, including in this volume, a consensus seems to be emerging that neither broad domains of practice—such as classroom management—nor very specific techniques or routines are to be understood as core practices. However, more research is needed on the underlying premise that targeting practices at this grain size is pedagogically effective.

Another definitional challenge related to grain size has to do with the comparisons between core practices and the competency-based movement of the 1970s, which was connected to microteaching. The pedagogy of rehearsing core practices is often conflated with microteaching in ways that may be problematic. Clearly, microteaching does represent one approximation of practice that also aims to advance teaching skills in specific situations. However, the theoretical basis underlying microteaching relied on more behavioral theories of learning in largely decontextualized classroom settings, whereas rehearsals of core practices, derived from a sociocultural perspective, much more strongly incorporate the respective individual and social circumstances and thus requires more adaptive action. The grain size of the techniques practiced in microteaching was often much narrower than the instructional routines and practices that are the basis of rehearsals. As the field progresses, it will be important to continue to define more precisely what constitutes a core practice and its components, as well as how best to teach core practices to both preservice and practicing teachers. This work will need to continue to be informed by research on teaching, including domain-specific research on teaching, and by theory on how people learn and develop expertise, including work from cognitive and social psychology and sociological work on learning in teams and small groups.[6]

Expanding the Research on How Best to Learn Core Practices

Another open question concerns how core practices can best be learned in higher education, given a university tradition that focuses primarily on generating and imparting theory. Even if professors embrace the notion of core practices as a way to integrate theory and practice, how are they best organized into a coherent curriculum for teacher learning? How can teacher educators sequence activities that engage learners in investigating and enacting these practices to support their ability to enact them in classroom settings? These questions are on the minds of many scholars around the world who are engaged in work around core practices.

The expectation of teacher educators to describe and represent core practices to increase their teachability and learnability also leads to the question whether the field of core practices should be more structured and conceptually organized. An important organizing principle is likely to be the extent to which core practices are relevant and effective for student learning. This may vary from subject to subject, and so each subject will set some emphases and prioritizations for itself, as is illustrated by a number of subject-specific frameworks for core practices.[7] For the Teaching-Works project's high-leverage practices, which name nineteen general practices, the order of most important practices derives from their relevance primarily to beginning and novice teachers.[8] Aebli's "Basic Forms of Teaching," which can be seen as an antecedent to the core practices, orders the practices according to the extent to which they can increasingly contribute to building mental structures in students.[9]

More recent work introduces interesting new approaches to organizing the introduction of core practices. For example, for teacher education, Hanna Westbroek and colleagues suggest introducing first those practices that are most important for coping with everyday teaching. Then, however, the learning needs of student teachers are included and goals are mutually agreed on; this results in individually tailored successions of how practices are introduced and rehearsed.[10] Klette and colleagues point to efforts around practice-based teacher education in Norway and show how core practices can be associated with higher-level domains of practice-based teacher education ("teaching and learning," "classroom management and relations," "assessment for learning," and "teaching for heterogonous classrooms") to create coherence at the program level.[11]

The desire for a common canon of core practices is understandable from the perspective of teacher education. However, it is important not to lose sight of the fact that core practices must be adapted to the local conditions of teacher education and the individual requirements of student teachers if they are to be successfully taught and applied. A number of efforts by teacher educators to build a curriculum around core practices have begun with the collective work of identifying those practices that teacher educators can agree are most important for their students; the work at the University of Connecticut illustrates this approach, and scholars have identified both the benefits and challenges of engaging colleagues in this work.[12]

Another open question has to do with how best to teach core practices in the context of the university. A productive approach, introduced by Pam Grossman and colleagues and refined by Morva McDonald and colleagues, identifies the framework that includes engaging in the representation, decomposition, and approximation of particular core practices in cycles of learning.[13] Many of the authors in this volume refer to this framework across both preservice and in-service teacher development, using the framework to inform their work with teachers. For example, building on the work of Elham Kazemi, Lynsey Gibbons and others, Kjersti Wæge and colleagues have experimented with time-outs in rehearsing core practices so that participants can discuss the processes and preferable next steps at the meta-level, and have explored the effects of this technique.[14] Alexander Groeschner and colleagues successfully use elaborate video labs in which student teachers can rehearse core practices which are captured in recordings that can be used for analysis and reflection.[15] Matthias Nückles and Marc Kleinknecht explore the sequencing of the different components of the learning cycle to understand whether the order of engaging in decompositions and deeper understanding of the components of practice affects novices' ability to enact the practices.[16]

However, other aspects also play a role in the acquisition of core practices by student teachers, such as which practices to focus on and when, and how to arouse and sustain student teachers' interest in practices. Student teachers vary in prior knowledge, current learning needs, and motivation. If core practices are to be learned successfully, it is necessary to be sensitive to these individual differences. This means that adaptivity must also be an essential feature of concepts and procedures for acquiring practices at the level of higher education.[17]

Another question raised by scholars has to do with the relative value of specifying core practices and whether or not such specifications constrain teachers' ability to tailor instruction for their own students. Klette and her colleagues raise the distinction between fidelity to prespecified practices versus more open-ended and flexible approaches to enactment.[18] As noted earlier, the goal of specification is to provide foundational and common understanding of the particular practices to be taught, with the expectation that as teachers develop their skill and understanding, they will use their professional expertise to adapt and tailor these practices to their particular contexts; from our perspective, the goal of adaptive expertise is a constituent feature of core practices.[19] However, as noted by literature on implementation research, questions might also be raised about at what point practices may be fundamentally altered in the process of adaptation, so that they no longer resemble the practices identified by research as effective in supporting student learning. There is also a pedagogical challenge for teacher education professionals in engaging with student teachers in a process of development and agreement that is open-ended and can lead to divergent but plausible practices, a dilemma that arises at the classroom level as well.[20] This is a tension that deserves further investigation.

The pedagogies of core practices that have been proposed in recent years seem plausible and have been shown to be effective in teacher education, but the research is still evolving.[21] In recent work, including in this volume, scholars have empirically examined the sequencing of activities such as representation and approximation for their effectiveness, as exemplified by Nückles and Kleinknecht, for example.[22] Other scholars are extending the work on preservice teacher education to professional development of teachers in settings that occur outside of a university course.[23] As the field develops, it will be important to share new pedagogical approaches, discuss experiences with them, and develop a programmatic approach to studying the effectiveness of different approaches.

Much of the extant work on core practices takes place within the context of formal preservice teacher education or professional development. Largely unaddressed is the self-organized learning of core practices, especially when prospective and in-service teachers are left on their own and do not receive regular feedback from professionals.[24] To what extent can teachers learn to enact these practices largely on their own in the context of their classrooms? As we know that novice teachers will continue to develop their repertoire of practices across their careers, how can we develop resources that support teachers' ability and willingness to continuously improve their core practices independently throughout their professional careers? Does an initial introduction to core practices early in one's career make teachers more receptive to continuing to develop and refine new practices? Can materials for practicing teachers be developed that provide them with the opportunity to see high-quality representations of a range of practices and guidance around enactment? Given the task of increasing the quality of teaching across the globe, questions of how to create materials for teachers and leaders to use within school contexts need greater attention.

MOVING FORWARD

This volume suggests that the concept of core practices has sparked a worldwide momentum in teacher education that is being sustained and fueled by an increasing number of scholars, researchers, and institutions. More and more teacher education programs are turning to practice-based teacher education, in recognition that too little theoretical knowledge finds its way into practice that is conducive and supportive to learning. In our own work with teachers, we've also seen evidence of how the concept of core practices is being embraced with great interest by practitioners and student teachers alike.

As more teacher educators in different countries around the world experiment with work concerning integrating core practices into teacher education, more and more questions are likely to arise that will require sustained investigation and collaboration. We are hopeful that this volume represents a first effort to identify some of the ways in which work on core practices is being taken up in different national contexts and the emerging research that is ongoing, as well as to raise questions for future deliberation and collaborative investigation.

NOTES

INTRODUCTION

1. See Fred Korthagen and J. P. Kessels, "Linking Theory and Practice: Changing the Pedagogy of Teacher Education," *Educational Researcher* 28, no. 4 (1999): 4–17; Deborah Loewenberg Ball and David K. Cohen, "Developing Practice, Developing Practitioners: Toward a Practice-Based Theory of Professional Education," in *Teaching as the Learning Profession: Handbook of Policy and Practice*, ed. Linda Darling-Hammond and G. Sykes (San Francisco: Jossey-Bass, 1999); Kenneth Zeichner, "The Turn Once Again Toward Practice-Based Teacher Education," *Journal of Teacher Education* 63, no. 5 (2012): 376–382.

2. C.f. Deborah Loewenberg Ball and Francesca M. Forzani, "The Work of Teaching and the Challenge for Teacher Education," *Journal of Teacher Education* 60, no. 5 (2009): 497–511; Pam Grossman, Karen Hammerness, and Morva McDonald, "Redefining Teaching, Re-imagining Teacher Education," *Teachers and Teaching: Theory and Practice* 15, no. 2 (2009): 273–289; Morva McDonald, Elham Kazemi, and Sarah Schneider Kavanagh, "Core Practices and Pedagogies of Teacher Education: A Call for a Common Language and Collective Activity," *Journal of Teacher Education* 64, no. 5 (2013): 378–386.

3. See, for example, Sarah Schneider Kavanagh, "Practice-Based Teacher Education: Surveying the Landscape, Considering Critiques, and Exploring Future Directions" (white paper for the Spencer Foundation, in press); Zeichner, "The Turn Once Again Toward Practice-Based Teacher Education."

4. Pam Grossman and Morva McDonald, "Back to the Future: Directions for Research in Teaching and Teacher Education," *American Educational Research Journal* 45, no. 1 (2008): 184–205; Pam Grossman, ed., *Teaching Core Practices in Teacher Education* (Cambridge, MA: Harvard Education Press, 2018).

5. Ball and Forzani, "The Work of Teaching and the Challenge for Teacher Education."

6. Angela Calabrese Barton, Edna Tan, and Daniel J. Birmingham, "Rethinking High-Leverage Practices in Justice-Oriented Ways," *Journal of Teacher Education* 71, no. 4 (2020): 477–494; Sarah Schneider Kavanagh and Katie A. Danielson, "Practicing Justice, Justifying Practice: Toward Critical Practice Teacher Education," *American Educational Research Journal* 57, no. 1 (2020): 69–105.

7. Giyoo Hatano and Kayoko Inagaki, "Two Courses of Expertise," in *Child Development and Education in Japan*, ed. H. Stevenson, H. Azuma, and K. Hakuta (New York: Freeman, 1986).

8. Mark Windschitl, Jessica Thompson, and Melissa Braaten, *Ambitious Science Teaching* (Cambridge MA: Harvard Education Press, 2018); Martin Nystrand et al., *Opening Dialogue: Understanding the Dynamics of Language and Learning in the English Classroom* (New York: Teachers College Press, 1997); Sarah Michaels, Catherine O'Connor, and Lauren B. Resnick, "Deliberative Discourse Idealized and Realized: Accountable Talk in the Classroom and in Civic Life," *Studies in Philosophy and Education* 27, no. 4 (2008): 283–297.

9. Bradley Fogo, "Core Practices for Teaching History: The Results of a Delphi Panel Survey," *Theory and Research in Social Education* 42, no. 2 (2014): 151–196; Pam Grossman et al., *Core Practices for Project-Based Learning: A Guide for Teachers and Leaders* (Cambridge, MA: Harvard University Press, 2021); Matthew Kloser, "Identifying a Core Set of Science Teaching Practices: A Delphi Expert Panel Approach," *Journal of Research in Science Teaching* 51, no. 9 (2014): 1185–1217. The identification of the nineteen high-leverage practices at TeachingWorks also involved a combination of reviewing the research literature and building professional consensus.

10. Calabrese Barton, Tan, and Birmingham, "Rethinking High-Leverage Practices in Justice-Oriented Ways."

11. Pam Grossman et al., "Teaching Practice: A Cross-Professional Perspective," *Teachers College Record* 111, no. 9 (2009): 2055–2100; Magdalene Lampert et al., "Keeping It Complex: Using Rehearsals to Support Novice Teacher Learning of Ambitious Teaching," *Journal of Teacher Education* 64, no. 3 (2013): 226–243; Elham Kazemi et al., "Getting Inside Rehearsals: Insights From Teacher Educators to Support Work on Complex Practice," *Journal of Teacher Education* 67, no. 1 (2016): 18–31; McDonald, Kazemi, and Kavanagh, "Core Practices and Pedagogies of Teacher Education."

12. Charles Goodwin, "Professional Vision," *American Anthropologist* 96 (1994): 606–633; Grossman et al., "Teaching Practice."

13. Lampert et al., "Keeping It Complex"; Elham Kazemi et al., "Getting Inside Rehearsals: Insights from Teacher Educators to Support Work on Complex Practice," *Journal of Teacher Education* 67, no. 1 (2016): 1–14; McDonald, Kazemi, and Kavanagh, "Core Practices and Pedagogies of Teacher Education."

14. Julia Cohen et al., "Teacher Coaching in a Simulated Environment," *Educational Evaluation and Policy Analysis* 42, no. 2 (2020): 208–231.

15. Schneider Kavanagh and Danielson, "Practicing Justice, Justifying Practice"; Thomas M. Philip et al., "Making Justice Peripheral by Constructing Practice

as 'Core': How the Increasing Prominence of Core Practices Challenges Teacher Education," *Journal of Teacher Education* 70, no. 3 (2018): 251–264.

16. Calabrese Barton, Tan, and Birmingham, "Rethinking High-Leverage Practices in Justice-Oriented Ways"; Schneider Kavanagh and Danielson, "Practicing Justice, Justifying Practice"; Philip et al., "Making Justice Peripheral by Constructing Practice as 'Core.'"

17. See, for example, Grossman, *Teaching Core Practices in Teacher Education*.

18. Thomas H. Levine et al., "Exploring the Nature, Facilitators, and Challenges of Program Coherence in a Case of Teacher Education Program Redesign Using Core Practices," *Journal of Teacher Education* 74, no. 1 (2022): 69–84.

19. Magdalena Muller, personal conversation, January 2017.

CHAPTER 1

1. Hans Aebli (1923–1990), professor at the Universities of Berlin, Konstanz, and Bern, was a Swiss theorist and researcher in the field of developmental and cognitive psychology, learning psychology, and didactics. Alongside his teacher education works, he engaged in making Jean Piaget more widely known, translated and published works by US cognitive psychologists such as Jerome Bruner, and authored a two-volume basic work on cognitive psychology (see endnote 16). For more information, see the website of the Aebli-Näf Foundation, accessed August 29, 2023, https://www.ans.ch/en/.

2. "High-Leverage Practices," TeachingWorks, accessed August 29, 2023, https://www.teachingworks.org/high-leverage-practices/.

3. The difficulty of translating the German word *Bildung* into other languages is pointed out by Jan Masschelein and Norbert Ricken, "Do We (Still) Need the Concept of Bildung?," *Educational Philosophy and Theory* 35, no. 2 (2003): "It seems to be tied very strongly to the particular history of Germany (both as the history of the formation and development of the nation and as the history of the German thought and language). One could use the word 'edification'; others use the term 'cultivation'" (151).

4. Jürgen Oelkers, "Entwicklungen der Lehrerbildung in Deutschland," in *Kulturen der Lehrerbildung in der Sekundarstufe in Italien und Deutschland: Nationale Formate und "cross culture,"* ed. Rita Casale et al. (Bad Heilbrunn: Klinkhardt, 2021), 262. This and all subsequent translations from German are by the authors.

5. Otto Friedrich Bollnow, "Theorie und Praxis in der Lehrerbildung," in *Die Theorie-Praxis-Diskussion in der Erziehungswissenschaft*, ed. Herwig Blankertz (Weinheim: Beltz, 1978), 164.

6. See Jürgen Oelkers, "Break and Continuity: Observations on the Modernization Effects and Traditionalization in International Reform Pedagogy," *Paedagogica Historica* 31, no. 3 (1995): 675–713.

7. In German, *didactics* is understood as a neutral term without negative connotations. The concept behind Didaktik encompasses both the reflection on *what* is taught (curriculum, syllabus) as well as on *how* it is taught—that is, the decisions on both the goals and content as well as the methodological dimension of teaching. Hanna Kiper, "Rezeption und Wirkung der Psychologischen Didaktik," in *Didaktik auf psychologischer Grundlage: Von Hans Aeblis kognitionspsychologischer Didaktik zur modernen Lehr- und Lernforschung*, ed. Matthias Baer et al. (Bern: HEP, 2006).

8. TIMSS (Trends in International Mathematics and Science Study) by the International Association for the Evaluation of Educational Achievement (IEA) and PISA (Programme for International Student Assessment) by the Organization for Economic Cooperation and Development (OECD) are both worldwide large-scale comparative studies of educational achievement.

9. Hans Aebli, "Ziele und Inhalte der erziehungswissenschaflichen und schulpraktischen Ausbildung von Berufsschullehrern mit einem ersten akademischen Abschluss (Diplom oder Lizentiat)," in *Wissenschaft und Praxis in der Berufsschullehrerbildung*, ed. K. Aregger (Aarau: Sauerländer, 1982).

10. Matthias Baer and Michael Fuchs, "Grundsätze der Lehrerinnen- und Lehrerbildung bei Hans Aebli," in Baer et al., *Didaktik auf psychologischer Grundlage*, 111.

11. Hans Aebli, *Didactique psychologique: Application à la didactique de la psychologie de Jean Piaget* (Neuchâtel: Delachaux et Niestlé, 1951).

12. For the term *didactics*, see endnote 7.

13. For a multifaceted view of Aebli's work on didactics and teacher education see Baer et al., ed., *Didaktik auf psychologischer Grundlage*.

14. Hans Aebli, *Psychologische Didaktik* (German translation of the 1951 French edition) (Stuttgart: Klett, 1963), 14–15.

15. Aebli, *Didactique psychologique: Application à la didactique de la psychologie de Jean Piaget*, 2.

16. Hans Aebli, *Denken, das Ordnen des Tuns. Bd. 1. Kognitive Aspekte der Handlungstheorie* (Stuttgart: Klett Cotta, 1980); Hans Aebli, *Denken, das Ordnen des Tuns. Bd. 2. Denkprozesse. Problemlösen und Begriffsbildung* (Stuttgart: Klett-Cotta, 1981).

17. Aebli, *Psychologische Didaktik*, 40.

18. Aebli, *Psychologische Didaktik*, 94.

19. Richard E. Mayer, "Should There Be a Three-Strikes Rule Against Pure Discovery Learning? The Case for Guided Methods of Instruction," *American Psychologist* 59, no. 1 (2004): 14–19.

20. See Sigmund Tobias and Thomas M. Duffy, *Constructivist Instruction: Success Or Failure?* (New York: Routledge, 2009); Christine Pauli and Kurt Reusser,

"Expertise in Swiss Mathematics Instruction," in *Expertise in Mathematics Instruction: An International Perspective*, ed. Yeping Li and Gabriele Kaiser (New York: Springer, 2011).

21. His work did not reach the Anglo-Saxon world, mainly because the publication of *Basic Forms of Teaching* in the 1970s and 1980s by a renowned US publisher failed due to difficulties in translation and adaptation for American readers.

22. Hans Aebli, *Zwölf Grundformen des Lernens: Eine Allgemeine Didaktik auf psychologischer Grundlage* (Stuttgart: Klett, 1983).

23. Joseph D. Novak and Alberto J. Cañas, "Theoretical Origins of Concept Maps, How to Construct Them, and Uses in Education," *Reflecting Education* 2, no. 1 (2007): 29–42.

24. Christine Pauli, "Fragend-entwickelnder Unterricht aus der Sicht der soziokulturalistisch orientierten Unterrichtsgesprächsforschung," in Baer et al., ed., *Didaktik auf psychologischer Grundlage*.

25. K. Anders Ericsson and Robert Pool, *Peak: Secrets from the New Science of Expertise* (Boston: Houghton Mifflin Harcourt, 2016).

26. Hans Aebli, *Grundlagen des Lehrens. Eine Allgemeine Didaktik auf psychologischer Grundlage* (Stuttgart: Klett-Cotta, 1987), 177–217.

27. Noam Chomsky, *Cartesian Linguistics: A Chapter in the History of Rationalist Thought* (New York: Harper & Row, 1966), 31–51.

28. Jasmin Decristan et al., "Oberflächen- und Tiefenmerkmale: Eine Reflexion zweier prominenter Begriffe der Unterrichtsforschung," in *Empirische Forschung zu Unterrichtsqualität: Theoretische Grundfragen und quantitative Modellierungen*, ed. Anna-Katharina Praetorius, Juliane Grünkorn, and Eckhard Klieme (Weinheim: Beltz Juventa, 2020), 102–116.

29. Aebli, *Zwölf Grundformen des Lernens*, 392.

30. Pam Grossman et al., "Teaching Practice: A Cross-Professional Perspective," *Teachers College Record* 111, no. 9 (2009): 2060.

31. Grossman et al., "Teaching Practice," 2058.

32. Morva McDonald, Elham Kazemi, and Sarah Schneider Kavanagh, "Core Practices and Pedagogies of Teacher Education: A Call for a Common Language and Collective Activity," *Journal of Teacher Education* 64, no. 5 (2013): 378–386.

33. These so-called training schools with normal classes and students ("Übungsschulen") as part of teacher education institutions have a tradition in the German-speaking world that goes back to the early nineteenth century.

34. Fritz Müller, ed., *Lehrerbildung von morgen: Grundlagen, Strukturen, Inhalte. Bericht der Expertenkommission im Auftrag der EDK* (Hitzkirch: Comenius, 1975), 186–192.

35. Aebli's concept of learning cycles was reflected in a nationwide study on the renewal of teacher education; see Fritz Müller, *Lehrerbildung von morgen.*

36. McDonald, Kazemi, and Kavanagh, "Core Practices and Pedagogies of Teacher Education."

CHAPTER 2

1. Morva McDonald, Elham Kazemi, and Sarah Schneider Kavanagh, "Core Practices and Pedagogies of Teacher Education: A Call for a Common Language and Collective Activity," *Journal of Teacher Education* 64, no. 5 (2013): 378–386, https://doi.org/10.1177/0022487113493807.

2. Fred Janssen, Pam Grossman, and Hanna Westbroek, "Facilitating Decomposition and Recomposition in Practice-Based Teacher Education: The Power of Modularity," *Teaching and Teacher Education* 51 (2015): 137–146, https://doi.org/10.1016/j.tate.2015.06.009.

3. Jean Lave and Etienne Wenger, *Situated Learning: Legitimate Peripheral Participation* (Cambridge: Cambridge University Press, 1991).

4. Maarten Vansteenkiste et al., "Identifying Configurations of Perceived Teacher Autonomy Support and Structure: Associations with Self-Regulated Learning, Motivation and Problem Behavior," *Learning and Instruction* 22 (2012): 431–439, https://doi.org/10.1016/j.learninstruc.2012.04.002.

5. Elisabeth Davis, "Characterizing Productive Reflection Among Preservice Elementary Teachers: Seeing What Matters," *Teaching and Teacher Education* 22, no. 3 (2006): 281–301, https://doi.org/10.1016/j.tate.2005.11.005.

6. Marilyn Cochran-Smith and Susan L. Lytle, *Inquiry as a Stance: Practitioner Research in the Next Generation* (New York: Teachers College Press, 2009).

7. Fred Janssen, Hanna Westbroek, and Walter Doyle, "Practicality Studies: How to Move from What Works in Principle to What Works in Practice," *Journal of the Learning Sciences* 24, no. 1 (2015): 176–186, https://doi.org/10.1080/10508406.2014.954751.

8. Harry Heft, "The Foundations of an Ecological Approach to Psychology," in *Handbook of Environmental and Conservation Psychology*, ed. Susan D. Clayton (Oxford: Oxford University Press, 2012), 1–40.

9. Mary M. Kennedy, "Attribution Error and the Quest for Teacher Quality," *Educational Researcher* 39, no. 8 (2010): 591–598, https://doi.org/10.3102/0013189X10390804.

10. Charles Carver, "Self-Awareness," in *Handbook of Self and Identity*, ed. Mark R. Leary and June P. Tangney (New York: Guilford Press, 2012), 50–69.

11. Hanna Westbroek et al., "Research Literacy in Initial Teacher Education: The Development of Personal Theories," in *Developing Teachers' Research Literacy: International Perspectives*, ed. Peter Boyd et al. (Libron: Kraków, 2021), 113.

12. Janssen, Grossman, and Westbroek, "Facilitating Decomposition and Recomposition," 137–146.

13. Pauline C. Meijer, Gitta de Graaf, and Jacobien Meirink, "Key Experiences in Student Teachers' Development," *Teachers and Teaching: Theory and Practice* 17, no. 1 (2011): 115–129, https://doi.org/10.1080/13540602.2011.538502.

14. Richard M. Ryan and Edward L. Deci, "Intrinsic and Extrinsic Motivation from a Self-Determination Theory Perspective: Definitions, Theory, Practices, and Future Directions," *Contemporary Educational Psychology* 61 (2020): 1–11, https://doi.org/10.1016/j.cedpsych.2020.101860.

15. Theo Wubbels et al., "Let's Make Things Better," in *Interpersonal Relationships In Education: An Overview of Contemporary Research*, ed. Theo Wubbels et al. (Rotterdam: Sense Publishers, 2012): 225–249.

16. Anja J. Doornbos, Sanneke Bolhuis, and Robert J. Simons, "Modeling Work-Related Learning on the Basis of Intentionality and Developmental Relatedness: A Non-educational Perspective," *Human Resource Development Review* 3, no. 3 (2004): 250–274, https://doi.org/ 10.1177/1534484304268107.

17. Fred Janssen et al., "How to Make Innovations Practical," *Teachers College Record* 115 (2013): 1–43, https://doi/10.1177/016146811311500703.

18. Westbroek et al., "Research Literacy in Initial Teacher Education," 113.

19. Janssen, Grossman, and Westbroek, "Facilitating Decomposition and Recomposition," 137–146.

20. Hanna B. Westbroek, Lisette van Rens, Ed van den Berg, and Fred Janssen, "A Practical Approach to Assessment for Learning and Differentiated Instruction," *International Journal of Science Education* 42, no. 6 (2020): 955–976, https://doi.org/10.1080/09500693.2020.1744044.

21. Mary K. Stein et al., "Orchestrating Productive Mathematical Discussions: Five Practices for Helping Teachers Move Beyond Show and Tell," *Mathematical Thinking and Learning* 10, no. 4 (2008): 313–340, https://doi.org/10.1080/10986060802229675.

22. Vansteenkiste et al., "Identifying Configurations," 431–439.

23. Janssen, Grossman, and Westbroek, "Facilitating Decomposition and Recomposition," 137–146.

24. Pam Grossman, Karen Hammerness, and Morva McDonald, "Redefining Teaching, Re-Imagining Teacher Education," *Teachers and Teaching: Theory and Practice* 15, no. 2 (2009): 273–289, https://doi.org/10.1080/13540600902875340.

CHAPTER 3

1. New South Wales Education Standards Authority, *Mathematics K–2* (Sydney: NSW Education Standards Authority, 2021).

2. Pamela Grossman, Karen Hammerness, and Morva McDonald, "Redefining Teaching, Re-imaging Teacher Education," *Teachers and Teaching: Theory and Practice* 15, no. 2 (2009): 273–289.

3. Peter Sullivan, Judy Mousley, and Robyn Zevenbergen, "Teacher Actions to Maximize Mathematics Learning Opportunities in Heterogeneous Classrooms," *International Journal of Science and Mathematics Education* 4 (2006): 117–143, https://doi.org/10.1007/s10763-005-9002-y.

4. Janette Bobis et al., "Instructional Moves That Increase Chances of Engaging All Students in Learning Mathematics," *Mathematics,* 9 (2021): 582, https://doi.org/10.3390/math9060582.

5. Organisation for Economic Co-operation Development, *Adapting Curriculum to Bridge Equity Gaps: Towards an Inclusive Curriculum* (Paris: OECD Publishing, 2021).

6. National Council of Teachers of Mathematics, *Principles to Actions: Ensuring Mathematical Success for All* (Reston, VA: National Council of Teachers of Mathematics, 2014); New South Wales Education Standards Authority, *Mathematics K–2.*

7. Sue Thomson et al., *PISA 2018: Reporting Australia's Results,* vol. 1, *Student Performance* (Melbourne: Australian Council for Educational Research, 2019), https://research.acer.edu.au/ozpisa/35.

8. Peter Sullivan et al., "Ways That Relentless Consistency and Task Variation Contribute to Teacher and Student Mathematics Learning," in *For the Learning of Mathematics: Proceedings of a Symposium on Learning in Honour of Laurinda Brown: Monograph 1,* ed. Alf Coles (New Westminster: FLM Publishing Association, 2020), 32.

9. Magdalene Lampert et al., "Keeping it Complex Using Rehearsals to Support Novice Teacher Training of Ambitious Teaching," *Journal of Teacher Education* 6 (2013): 241, https://doi.org/10.1177/0022487112473837.

10. Glen Fahey, Jordan O'Sullivan, and Jared Bussell, "Failing to Teach the Teacher: An Analysis of Mathematics Initial Teacher Education" (Analysis Paper 29), Centre for Independent Studies, Sydney, 2021.

11. "Australian Professional Standards for Teachers," last modified 2018, https://www.aitsl.edu.au/standards.

12. Glenda Anthony, Andrea Cooke, and Tracey Muir, "Challenges, Reforms, and Learning in Initial Teacher Education," in *Research in Mathematics Education in Australasia 2012–2015,* ed. Katie Makar et al. (Singapore: Springer, 2016), 305–327.

13. Charalambos Charalambous et al., "Learning to Teach Ambitiously: A Multiple Case Study of Practising Teachers' Experimentation with Enables

and Extenders," *Journal of Mathematics Teacher Education* 26 (2023): 363–394, https://doi.org/10.1007/s10857-022-09532-9.

14. James Russo et al., "Using Enabling and Extending Prompts in the Early Primary Years When Teaching with Sequences of Challenging Mathematical Tasks," *Proceedings of the 44th Annual Conference of the Mathematics Education Research Group of Australasia*, July 3–7, 2022 (Launceston: Mathematics Education Research Group of Australasia, 2022), 482–489.

15. Russo et al., "Using Enabling and Extending Prompts," 482–489.

16. Jay Jennings and Kasia Muldner, "Assistance That Fades In Improves Learning Better Than Assistance That Fades Out," *Instructional Science* 48 (2020): 371–394, https://doi.org/10.1007/s11251-020-09520-7.

17. Russo et al., "Using Enabling and Extending Prompts," 482–489.

18. Jill Cheeseman, Ann Downton, and Sharyn Livy, "Investigating Teachers' Perceptions of Enabling and Extending Prompts," *Proceedings of the 40th Annual Conference of the Mathematics Education Research Group of Australasia* (Melbourne: Mathematics Education Research Group of Australasia, 2017), 141–148.

19. Doug Clarke et al., "Teaching Strategies for Building Student Persistence on Challenging Tasks: Insights Emerging from Two Approaches to Teacher Professional Learning," *Mathematics Teacher Education and Development* 16, no. 2 (2014): 46–70.

20. Louise Hodgson, "Seeing Is Not Enough for Believing: Building Mathematical Knowledge for Teaching Through Observing, Deconstructing, and Enacting Particular Pedagogies" (PhD diss., Monash University, 2019).

21. Charalambous et al., "Learning to Teach Ambitiously," 29.

22. Charalambous et al., "Learning to Teach Ambitiously," 29; Cheeseman et al., "Investigating Teachers' Perceptions," 141–148; Russo et al., "Using Enabling and Extending Prompts," 482–489.

23. Janette Bobis and Kristen Tripet, "Situating Teacher Learning in the Mathematics Classroom and Everyday Practice," in *International Encyclopedia of Education*, ed. Robert Tierney et al. (Oxford: Elsevier, 2023).

24. Ralph Putnam and Hilda Borko, "What Do New Views of Knowledge and Thinking Have to Say About Research on Teacher Learning?," *Educational Researcher* 29, no. 1 (2000): 4–15, https://doi.org/10.3102/0013189X029001004.

25. Elham Kazemi and Allison Hintz, *Intentional Talk: How to Lead Productive Mathematical Discussions* (Portland: Stenhouse Publishers, 2014).

26. Jennifer Fereday and Eimear Muir-Cochrane, "Demonstrating Rigor Using Thematic Analysis: A Hybrid Approach of Inductive and Deductive Coding and Theme Development," *International Journal of Qualitative Methods* 5, no. 1 (2006): 80–92.

27. Jennings and Muldner, "Assistance That Fades In," 371–394.
28. Hodgson, "Seeing Is Not Enough for Believing."
29. Hodgson, "Seeing Is Not Enough for Believing."
30. Organisation for Economic Co-operation Development, *Adapting Curriculum to Bridge Equity Gaps* (Paris: OECD Publishing, 2021).
31. Jodie Hunter et al., "Innovative and Powerful Pedagogical Practices in Mathematics Education," in *Research in Mathematics Education in Australasia 2016–2019*, ed. Jennifer Way et al. (Singapore: Springer, 2020).

CHAPTER 4

1. Linda Darling-Hammond, *Powerful Teacher Education: Lessons from Exemplary Programs* (San Francisco: Jossey-Bass, 2006); Pam Grossman, Karen Hammerness, and Morva McDonald, "Redefining Teaching, Re-imagining Teacher Education," *Teachers and Teaching: Theory and Practice* 15, no. 2 (2009): 273–290, https://doi.org/10.1080/13540600902875340; Karen Hammerness et al., "Opportunities to Study, Practice, and Rehearse Teaching in Teacher Preparation: An International Perspective," *Teachers College Record* 122, no. 11 (2020): 1–46, https://doi.org/10.1177/016146812012201108.
2. Karen Hammerness et al., "Opportunities to Study"; Morva McDonald, Elham Kazemi, and Sarah Kavanagh, "Core Practices and Pedagogies of Teacher Education: A Call for a Common Language and Collective Activity," *Journal of Teacher Education* 64, no. 5 (2013): 378–386, https://doi.org/10.1177/0022487113493807; Tricia L. DeGraff, Cynthia M. Schmidt, and Jennifer H. Waddell, "Field-Based Teacher Education in Literacy: Preparing Teachers in Real Classroom Contexts," *Teaching Education* 26, no. 4 (2015): 366–382.
3. Core Practice Consortium, 2023, https://www.corepracticeconsortium.org/.
4. Mary Kennedy, "Parsing the Practice of Teaching," *Journal of Teacher Education* 67, no. 1 (2016): 6–17, https://doi.org/10.1177/0022487115614617.
5. Esther T. Canrinus, Kirsti Klette, and Karen Hammerness, "Diversity in Coherence: Strengths and Opportunities of Three Programs," *Journal of Teacher Education* 70, no. 3 (2019): 192–205, https://doi.org/10.1177/0022487117737305; Grossman, Hammerness, and McDonald, "Redefining Teaching."
6. As argued, the way we use *core practices* in this chapter refers to a rather broad definition of the term and includes what Deborah Ball and Francesca Forzani termed "high-leverage practices" (they distinguished among nineteen distinct high-leverage practices), in "Building a Common Core for Learning to Teach, and Connecting Professional Learning to Practice," *American Educator* 35, no. 2 (2001): 17–21, https://files.eric.ed.gov/fulltext/EJ931211.pdf; and what

Magdalene Lampert, Megan Loef Franke, Elham Kazemi, Hala Ghousseini, Angela Chan Turrou, Heather Beasley, Adrian Cunard, and Kathleen Crowe named "ambitious teaching," in "Keeping It Complex: Using Rehearsals to Support Novice Teacher Learning of Ambitious Teaching," *Journal of Teacher Education* 64, no. 3 (2013): 226–243, https://doi.org/10.1177 /0022487112473837.

7. Dana Grosser-Clarkson and Michael A. Neel, "Contrast, Commonality, and a Call for Clarity: A Review of the Use of Core Practices in Teacher Education," *Journal of Teacher Education* 71, no. 4 (2020): 71, https://doi.org/10.1177 /0022487119880162.

8. Elham Kazemi, "Teaching a Mathematics Methods Course: Understanding Learning from a Situated Perspective," in *Building Support for Scholarly Practices in Mathematics Methods*, ed. Signe E. Kastberg et al. (Charlotte, NC: Information Age Publishing, 2017), 49–69; Kristi J. Davin and Amy J. Heineke, "Preparing Teacher for Language Assessment: A Practice-Based Approach," *TESOL Journal* 7, no. 4 (2016): 921–938.

9. Grossman, Hammerness, and McDonald, "Redefining Teaching."

10. Pam Grossman, Sarah Kavanagh, and Christopher Dean, "The Turn Towards Practice in Teacher Education," in *Teaching Core Practices in Teacher Education*, ed. Pam Grossman (Cambridge, MA: Harvard Education Press, 2018), 1–14; Kirsti Klette, "Classroom Observation as a Means of Understanding Teaching Quality: Towards a Shared Language of Teaching?," *Journal of Curriculum Studies* (submitted for publication, 2022).

11. Pam Grossman et al., "Teaching Practice: A Cross-Professional Perspective," *Teachers College Record* 111, no. 9 (2009): 2055–2100.

12. Inga S. Jenset, Kirsti Klette, and Karen Hammerness, "Grounding Teacher Education in Practice Around the World: An Examination of Teacher Education Coursework in Teacher Education Programs in Finland, Norway, and the United States," *Journal of Teacher Education* 69, no. 2 (2018): 184–197, https://doi.org/10.1177/0022487117728248.

13. Katie A. Danielson, Meghan Shaughnessy, and Lightning Peter Jay, "Use of Representation in Teacher Education," in *Teaching Core Practices in Teacher Education*, ed. Pam Grossman. (Cambridge, MA: Harvard Education Press, 2018), 15–34.

14. Kristine M. Schutz, Pam Grossman, and Meghan Shaughnessy, "Approximations of Practice in Teacher Education," in *Teaching Core Practices in Teacher Education*, ed. Pam Grossman (Cambridge, MA: Harvard Education Press, 2018), 57–85.

15. DeGraff, Schmidt, and Waddell, "Field-Based Teacher Education"; Jenset, Klette, and Hammerness, "Grounding Teacher Education."

16. Grossman et al., "Teaching Practice"; Grossman, Hammerness, and McDonald, "Redefining Teaching."

17. Marieke Van der Schaaf et al., "Evidence for Measuring Teachers' Core Practices," *European Journal of Teacher Education* 42, no. 5 (2019), 675–694, https://doi.org/10.1080/02619768.2019.1652903.

18. McDonald, Kazemi, and Kavanagh, "Core Practices and Pedagogies"; Kiomi Matsumoto-Royo and María S. Ramírez-Montoya, "Core Practices in Practice-Based Teacher Education: A Systematic Literature Review of its Teaching and Assessment Process," *Studies in Educational Evaluation* 70 (2021), https://doi .org/10.1016/j.stueduc.2021.101047.

19. Matsumoto-Royo and Ramírez-Montoya, "Core Practices."

20. Van der Schaaf et al., "Evidence for Measuring."

21. Canrinus, Klette, and Hammerness, "Diversity in Coherence"; Linda Darling-Hammond et al., "The Design of Teacher Education Programs," in *Preparing Teachers for a Changing World. What Teachers Should Know and be Able to Do*, ed. Linda Darling-Hammond and John Bransford (San Francisco: Jossey-Bass, 2005); Karen Hammerness, "From Coherence in Theory to Coherence in Practice," *Teachers College Record* 108, no. 7 (2006): 1241–1265; Lampert et al., "Keeping It Complex."

22. Hammerness, "From Coherence in Theory." In the literature, people also point to institutional coherence (Hermansen, Hege, "In Pursuit of Coherence: Aligning Program Development in Teacher Education with Institutional Practices," *Scandinavian Journal of Educational Research* 64, no. 6: 936–952, https://doi.org/10.1080/00313831.2019.1639815) and biographical and transitional coherence (Jens-Christian Smeby and Kåre Heggen, "Gir Mest Mulig Samanheng Også Den Beste Profesjonsutdanninga?" [Does More Coherence Give the Better Professional Education?], *Norsk pedagogisk tidsskrift*, no. 1 (2012): 4–13, http://www.idunn.no/ts/npt/2012/01/art05). However, as we see the term *coherence*, the distinction between conceptual and structural coherence embodies the main features of coherence with regard to program design, and these other facets of coherence do not bring any new and critical aspects to the conceptual discussion.

23. Hammerness, "From Coherence in Theory"; Karen Hammerness, "A Comparative Study of Three Key Features in the Design and Practice of Teacher Education in the United States and Norway: Part I. Findings from a Study in the United States," *VISIONS 2011: Teacher Education* 6 (2012).

24. Hammerness, "Comparative Study," 3

25. Hammerness, "From Coherence in Theory."

26. Grossman et al., "Teaching Practice," 282.

27. Karen Hammerness and Kirsti Klette, "Indicators of Quality in Teacher Education: Looking at Features of Teacher Education from an International Perspective," in *Promoting and Sustaining a Quality Teaching Workforce*, vol. 27, ed. Alexander W. Wiseman and Gerald K. LeTendre (Bingley, UK: Emerald Group Publishing, 2015), 8.

28. Thomas H. Levine et al., "Exploring the Nature, Facilitators, and Challenges of Program Coherence in a Case of Teacher Education Program Redesign Using Core Practices," *Journal of Teacher Education* 74, no. 1 (2022): 69–84, https://doi.org/10.1177/00224871221108645.

29. Levine et al., "Exploring the Nature," 12.

30. Meredith I. Honig and Thomas C. Hatch, "Crafting Coherence: How Schools Strategically Manage Multiple, External Demands," *Educational Researcher* 33, no. 8 (2004): 16–30; Canrinus, Klette, and Hammerness, "Diversity in Coherence"; Levine et al., "Exploring the Nature," 3.

31. In addition, there is a bachelor's program for teachers in preschools and several programs for teachers of vocational subjects as well as of some specific subjects, such as physical education and arts. Advisory Panel for Teacher Education (APT), *Transforming Norwegian Teacher Education: The Final Report for the International Advisory Panel for Primary and Lower Secondary Teacher Education* (2020), https://www.nokut.no/globalassets/nokut/rapporter/ua /2020/transforming-norwegian-teacher-education-2020.pdf .

32. For more information about recent developments in teacher education pathways in Norway, see APT, *Transforming Norwegian Teacher Education*.

33. APT, *Transforming Norwegian Teacher Education*; Håkon Finne, Siri Mordal, and Trine Marie Stene, *Oppfatninger av studiekvalitet i lærerutdanningene 2013 [Perceived study quality in teacher education 2013]*, SINTEF, 2014, https://sintef .brage.unit.no/sintef-xmlui/handle/11250/2562981; Norwegian Agency for Quality Assurance in Education (NOKUT), *Evaluering av allmennlærerutdannin- gen i Norge 2006. Del 1: Hovedrapport [Evaluation of general teacher education in Norway 2006. Part 1: Main report]* (2006), https://www.nokut.no/contentassets /40568ec86aab411ba43c5a880ae339b5/alueva_hovedrapport.pdf.

34. Norwegian Ministry of Education, *National Curriculum for Teacher Education Grades 8–13*, (2013), https://lovdata.no/dokument/SF/forskrift/2013-03-18-288.

35. Kari Smith, "The Role of Research in Teacher Education," *Research in Teacher Education* 5, no. 2 (2015): 43–46, https://doi.org/10.15123/PUB.4767; Anna-Lena Østern, "Responding to the Challenge of Providing Stronger Research Base for Teacher Education: Research Discourses in the Norwegian National Research School for Teacher Education," *Educational Research* 58, no. 1 (2016): 73–90, https://doi.org/10.1080/00131881.2015.1129116.

36. Elaine Munthe and Peder Haug, "Research on Teacher Education in Norway 2000–2009: Trends and Gaps," EARLI conference, Amsterdam, The Netherlands (2009); Elaine Munthe, Kari-Anne Svensen Malmo & Magne Rogne, "Teacher Education Reform and Challenges in Norway," *Journal of Education for Teaching* 37, no. 4 (2011): 441–450, https://doi.org/10.1080/02607476.2011.611012; Norwegian Agency for Quality Assurance in Education (NOKUT), *Evaluering av lektorutdanningene: Spørreundersøkelse blant lektorstudenter; Hvordan opplever de utdanningen sin?* (2021), https://www.nokut.no/globalassets/nokut/rapporter /ua/2021/evaluering-av-lektorutdanningene_sporreundersokelse-blant -lektorstudenter_7-2021.pdf; Østern, "Responding to the Challenge."

37. Andreas Lund and Tone M. Eriksen, "Teacher Education as Transformation: Some Lessons Learned from a Center for Excellence in Education," *Acta Didactica Norge* 10, no. 2. (2016): 53–72, https://www.journals.uio.no/index .php/adno/article/view/2483/2458.; Karin Rørnes, "Universitetsskoler I Lærerutdanningen: Å Koble Praksis Og Teori I Lærerutdanningen" [University Schools in Teacher Education: Connecting Practice and Theory in Teacher Education], in *Veier Til Fremragende Lærerutdanning* [Roads Towards Excellent Teacher Education], ed. Ulrikke Rindal, Andreas Lund, and Rachel Jakhelln (Oslo, Norway: Universitetsforlaget, 2015), 75–86.

38. Lund, Jakhelln, and Rindal, *Veier Til Fremragende Lærerutdanning.*

39. Kirsti Klette et al., *Fagvisjoner I Pedagogisk Praksis: Program for Utdanning Av Pedagogiske Faglærere Ved ILS (Pupils). Sluttrapport Fra Utredningskomitéen for En Modell for Fornying Av Lærerutdanningen Ved Institutt for Lærerutdanning Og Skoleforskning Ved UiO* [Visions for Pedagogical Practice: Program for the Education of Teachers at ILS (Pupils). Final Report from the Committee for the Development of Teacher Education at ILS]. Oslo, Norway: Department of Teacher Education and School Research, University of Oslo, 2011), http:// www.uv.uio.no/ils/studier/kvalitet/pupils/pupils-rapport.pdf.

40. For full description of the data from the smaller case studies, see Gøril Brataas and Inga S. Jenset, "From Coursework Intervention to Fieldwork: Using Video to Support Teacher Candidates' Reasoning and Enactment of Three Practices for Instructional Scaffolding" (manuscript submitted for publication, 2023); Canrinus, Klette, and Hammerness, "Diversity in Coherence"; Inga S. Jenset and Marte Blikstad-Balas, "Ny praksisform i lærerutdanningen: Analysepraksis for forsknings- og profesjonsforberedelse," *Acta Didactica Norden (ADNO)* (2022), https://journals.uio.no/adnorden/index.

41. Grosser-Clarkson and Neel, "Contrast, Commonality, and a Call."

42. Canrinus, Klette, and Hammerness, "Diversity in Coherence"; Hammerness, "From Coherence in Theory"; Hammerness and Klette, "Indicators of Quality"; Levine et al., "Exploring the Nature."

43. Levine et al., "Exploring the Nature."

44. Karen Littleton and Niel Mercer, *Interthinking: Putting Talk to Work* (New York: Routledge, 2013).

45. Inga S. Jenset et al., "The Oslo PROF Model: A Case of Research-Based Reform Efforts in Teacher Education" (manuscript submitted for publication, 2023).

46. Norwegian Agency for Quality Assurance in Education (NOKUT), *Sluttrapport fra evalueringen av lektorutdanning for trinn 8–13 [Evaluation of integrated five-year teacher education for 8-13. Final report]*, 2022, 57–61, https://www .nokut.no/globalassets/nokut/rapporter/ua/2022/sluttrapport-fra-nokuts -evaluering-av-lektorutdanning-for-trinn-813_15-2022.pdf.

47. Grosser-Clarkson and Neel, "Contrast, Commonality, and a Call."

48. Ronald F. Ferguson, *Student Perceptions of Teaching Effectiveness* (discussion brief), National Center for Teacher Effectiveness and the Achievement Gap Initiative, Harvard University, 2010.

49. Van der Schaaf et al., "Evidence for Measuring."

50. Cyrille Gaudin and Sébastien Chaliès, "Video Viewing in Teacher Education and Professional Development: A Literature Review," *Educational Research Review* 16 (2015): 41–67, https://doi.org/10.1016/j.edurev.2015.06.001; Rosella Santagata et al., "Mathematics Teacher Learning to Notice: A Systematic Review of Studies of Video-Based Programs," *ZDM—Mathematics Education* 53, no. 1 (2021): 119–134, https://doi.org/10.1007/s11858-020-01216-z.

51. Inga S. Jenset and Marte Blikstad-Balas, "Ny praksisform i lærerutdanningen: Analysepraksis for forsknings- og profesjonsforberedelse," *Acta Didactica Norden* 15, no. 3 (2021): 23, https://doi.org/10.5617/adno.8153.

52. Thomas J. Kane and Douglas O. Staiger, *Gathering Feedback for Teaching Combining High-Quality Observations with Student Surveys and Achievement Gains*, Bill and Melinda Gates Foundation, 2012, https://files.eric.ed.gov /fulltext/ED540960.pdf; Kirsti Klette and Marte Blikstad-Balas, "Observation Manuals as Lenses to Classroom Teaching: Pitfalls and Possibilities," *European Educational Research Journal* 17, no. 1 (2018): 129–146, https://doi.org /10.1177/1474904117703228.

53. Pam Grossman et al., "Measure for Measure: The Relationship Between Measures of Instructional Practice in Middle School English Language Arts and Teachers' Value-Added Scores," *American Journal of Education* 119, no. 3 (2013): 445–470; Julie Cohen, "Practices That Cross Disciplines? Revisiting Explicit Instruction in Elementary Mathematics and English Language Arts," *Teaching and Teacher Education* 69 (2018): 324–335, https://doi.org/10.1016 /j.tate.2017.10.021; Camilla G. Magnusson, Astrid Roe, and Marte Blikstad-Balas, "To What Extent and How Are Reading Comprehension Strategies Part of Language Arts Instruction? A Study of lower Secondary Classrooms,"

Reading Research Quarterly 54, no. 2 (2019): 187–212., https://doi.org /https://doi.org/10.1002/rrq.231; Michael Tengberg et al., "The Quality of Instruction in Swedish Lower Secondary Language Arts and Mathematics," *Scandinavian Journal of Educational Research* (2021), https://doi.org /10.1080/00313831.2021.1910564.

54. Brataas and Jenset, "From Coursework Intervention to Fieldwork."

55. Brataas and Jenset, "From Coursework Intervention to Fieldwork"; Klette, "Classroom Observation"; McDonald, Kazemi, and Kavanagh, "Core Practices and Pedagogies."

56. Mieke Lunenberg, "Characteristics, Scholarship and Research of Teacher Educators," in *International Encyclopedia of Education* (3rd ed.), ed. Penelope Peterson, Eva Baker, and Barry McGaw (Oxford: Elsevier, 2010), 676–680.

57. Sarah Kavanagh, Jenni Conrad, and Sarah Dagogo-Jack, "From Rote to Reasoned: Examining the Role of Pedagogical Reasoning in Practice-Based Teacher Education," *Teaching and Teacher Education* 89, no. 4 (2020): 1029912020, https://doi.org/10.1016/j.tate.2019.102991; Mary Kennedy, "Parsing the Practice"; Thomas M. Philip et. al., "Making Justice Peripheral by Constructing Practice as 'Core': How the Increasing Prominence of Core Practices Challenges Teacher Education," *Journal of Teacher Education* 70, no. 3 (2019): 251–264, https://doi.org/10.1177/0022487118798324.

58. Levine et al., "Exploring the Nature," 12.

59. Grosser-Clarkson and Neel, "Contrast, Commonality, and a Call."

CHAPTER 5

1. Ewald Terhart, "Critical Overview of Teacher Education in Germany," in *Oxford Research Encyclopedia of Education*, ed. George W. Noblit (New York: Oxford University Press, 2019), 1–22.

2. Fred A. Korthagen, "How Teacher Education Can Make a Difference," *Journal of Education for Teaching* 36, no. 4 (2010): 407–423, https://doi.org/10.1080 /02607476.2010.513854.

3. See Core Practice Consortium, home page, last modified 2023, https://www .corepracticeconsortium.org/.

4. For example, Benjamin Fauth et al., "Student Ratings of Teaching Quality in Primary School: Dimensions and Prediction of Student Outcomes," *Learning and Instruction* 29 (2014): 1–9, https://doi.org/10.1016/j.learninstruc.2013.07.001; Eckhard Klieme, Christine Pauli, and Kurt Reusser, "The Pythagoras Study: Investigating Effects of Teaching and Learning in Swiss and German Mathematics Classrooms," in *The Power of Video Studies in Investigating Teaching and Learning in the Classroom*, ed. Tomáš Janik and Tina Seidel (Münster: Waxmann, 2009), 137–160. For a critical discussion, see Matthias Nückles, "Investigating

Visual Perception in Teaching and Learning Using Eye-Tracking Methodology: Rewards and Challenges of an Innovative Research Paradigm," *Educational Psychology Review* 33, no. 1 (2021): 149–167, https://doi.org/10.1007/s10648 -020-09567-5.

5. Pam Grossman, Karen Hammerness, and Morva McDonald, "Redefining Teaching, Re-imagining Teacher Education," *Teachers and Teaching: Theory and Practice* 15 (2009): 273–289, https://doi.org/10.1080/13540600902875340. See also Morva McDonald, Elham Kazemi, and Sarah Schneider Kavanagh, "Core Practices and Pedagogies of Teacher Education: A Call for a Common Language and Collective Activity," *Journal of Teacher Education* 64, no. 5 (2013): 378–386, https://doi.org/10.1177/0022487113493807.

6. Jere E. Brophy and Thomas L. Good, "Teacher Behavior and Student Achievement," in *Handbook of Research on Teaching* (3rd ed.), ed. Merlin C. Wittrock (New York: Macmillan, 1986), 328–357; David C. Berliner, "The Place of Process-Product Research in Developing the Agenda for Research on Teacher Thinking," *Educational Psychologist* 24 (1989): 325–344, https://doi.org /10.1207/s15326985ep2404_1.

7. McDonald, Kazemi, and Kavanagh, "Core Practices and Pedagogies."

8. John R. Anderson, "Acquisition of Cognitive Skill," *Psychological Review* 89 (1989): 369, https://doi.org/10.1037/0033-295X.89.4.369; Manu Kapur, "Productive Failure," *Cognition and Instruction* 26, no. 3 (2008): 379–424, https://doi.org/10.1080/¬07370000802212669.

9. Annemarie Sullivan Palinscar and Ann L. Brown, "Reciprocal Teaching of Comprehension-Fostering and Comprehension-Monitoring Activities," *Cognition and Instruction* 1 (1984): 117–175, https://doi.org/10.1207 /s1532690xci0102_1.

10. Douglas Hacker and Arnette Tenent, "Implementing Reciprocal Teaching in the Classroom: Overcoming Obstacles and Making Modifications," *Journal of Educational Psychology* 94, no. 4 (2002): 699–718, https://doi.org/10.1037 /0022-0663.94.4.699; Barak Rosenshine and Carla Meister, "Reciprocal Teaching: A Review of the Research," *Review of Educational Research* 64 (1994): 479–530, https://doi.org/10.3102/00346543064004479; Nina Schünemann et al., "Peer Feedback Mediates the Impact of Self-Regulation Procedures on Strategy Use and Reading Comprehension in Reciprocal Teaching Groups," *Instructional Science* 45, no. 4 (2017): 395–415, https://doi.org/10.1007 /s11251-017-9409-1.

11. Rosenshine and Meister, "Reciprocal Teaching."

12. See Allan Collins, John S. Brown, and Susan E. Newman, "Cognitive Apprenticeship: Teaching the Craft of Reading, Writing, and Mathematics," in *Knowing, Learning, and Instruction: Essays in Honor of Robert Glaser,*

ed. Lauren B. Resnick (Hillsdale, NJ: Lawrence Erlbaum Associates, 1989), 453–494.

13. See Anat Zohar and Bracha Peled, "The Effects of Explicit Teaching of Metastrategic Knowledge on Low- and High-Achieving Students," *Learning and Instruction* 18 (2008): 337–353, https://doi.org/10.1016/j.learninstruc .2007.07.001.

14. McDonald, Kazemi, and Kavanagh, "Core Practices and Pedagogies."

15. McDonald, Kazemi, and Kavanagh, "Core Practices and Pedagogies."

16. For a summary, see John R. Anderson and Christian D. Schunn, "Implications of the ACT-R Learning Theory: No Magic Bullets," in *Advances in Instructional Psychology: Educational Design and Cognitive Science*, vol. 5, ed. Robert Glaser (Mahwah, NJ: Lawrence Erlbaum Associates, 2000): 1–33.

17. Jacob S. Kounin, *Discipline and Group Management in Classrooms* (New York: Holt, Rinehart & Winston, 1970).

18. See Nückles, "Investigating Visual Perception."

19. McDonald, Kazemi, and Kavanagh, "Core Practices and Pedagogies."

20. Kapur, "Productive Failure."

21. For a review, see Katharina Loibl, Ido Roll, and Nikol Rummel, "Towards a Theory of When and How Problem Solving Followed by Instruction Supports Learning," *Educational Psychology Review* 29 (2017): 693–715, https://doi.org /10.1007/s10648-016-9379-x.

22. Mary M. Kennedy, "The Role of Preservice Teacher Education," in *Teaching as the Learning Profession: Handbook of Teaching and Policy*, ed. Linda Darling-Hammond and Gary Sykes (San Francisco: Jossey Bass, 1999): 54–86.

23. McDonald, Kazemi, and Kavanagh, "Core Practices and Pedagogies."

24. Inga Glogger et al., "Inventing Prepares Computer-Based Learning in Student Teachers Motivationally and Cognitively," *Journal of Computer Assisted Learning*, 31 (2015): 546–561, https://doi.org/10.1111/jcal.12097.

25. Grossman, Hammerness, and McDonald, "Redefining Teaching."

26. McDonald, Kazemi, and Kavanagh, "Core Practices and Pedagogies."

27. Christopher N. Prilop, Kira E. Weber, and Marc Kleinknecht, "Effects of Digital Video-Based Feedback Environments on Pre-service Teachers' Feedback Competence," *Computers in Human Behavior* 102 (2020): 120–131, https://doi.org/10.1016/¬j.chb.2019.08.011.

28. Funded by the German Research Association, Project No. 491157666.

29. Glogger et al., "Inventing Prepares Computer-Based Learning."

30. Broß, "Förderung des Erwerbs von Core Practices."

31. Loibl, Roll, and Rummel, "Towards a Theory."

32. Kapur, "Productive Failure."

33. Kennedy, "Role of Preservice Teacher Education."

34. McDonald, Kazemi, and Kavanagh, "Core Practices and Pedagogies."

35. Cyrille Gaudin and Sébastien Chaliès, "Video Viewing in Teacher Education and Professional Development: A Literature Review," *Educational Research Review* 16 (2015): 41–67, https://doi.org/10.1016/j.edurev.2015.06.001; Nückles, "Investigating Visual Perception."

36. McDonald, Kazemi, and Kavanagh, "Core Practices and Pedagogies"; Grossman, Hammerness, and McDonald, "Redefining Teaching." The empirical research reported in this chapter was supported by the Federal Ministry of Education and Research in Germany (BMBF) as part of the second funding phase of the "Quality Offensive in German Teacher Education" (2019–2023). All presented data were collected by Imke Broß under the supervision of Matthias Nückles and Anja Prinz as partial fulfillment of the requirements for Imke Broß's PhD at the University of Freiburg, Faculty of Economic and Behavioral Sciences.

CHAPTER 6

1. Part of the research reported in this chapter regarding the Learning-to-Teach Lab: Science is funded by the German Federal Ministry of Education and Research (Grant No. 01JA1808). We thank all collaborators of our studies reported in this chapter and our partners at universities and schools.

2. Verena Jurik, Alexander Gröschner, and Tina Seidel, "How Student Characteristics Affect Girls' and Boys' Verbal Engagement in Physics Instruction," *Learning and Instruction* 23 (2013): 33–42; Sue Lyle, "Dialogic Teaching: Discussing Theoretical Contexts and Reviewing Evidence from Classroom Practice," *Language and Education* 22, no. 3 (2008): 222–240.

3. See Christine Howe and Manzoorul Abedin, "Classroom Dialogue: A Systematic Review Across Four Decades of Research," *Cambridge Journal of Education* 43, no. 3 (2013): 325–356; Neil Mercer, Rupert Wegerif, and Louis Major, eds., *Routledge International Handbook of Research on Dialogic Education* (London: Routledge, 2020); Valentina Guzmán and Antonia Larrain, "The Transformation of Pedagogical Practices into Dialogic Teaching: Towards a Dialogic Notion of Teacher Learning," *Professional Development in Education* (2021), https://doi.org/10.1080/19415257.2021.1902837; Klara Sedova et al., eds., *Getting Dialogic Teaching into Classrooms* (Singapore: Springer, 2020); Chiel van der Veen et al., "The Effect of Productive Classroom Talk and Metacommunication on Young Children's Oral Communicative Competence and Subject Matter Knowledge: An Intervention Study in Early Childhood Education," *Learning and Instruction* 48 (2017): 14–22.

4. Robin Alexander, "Developing Dialogic Teaching: Genesis, Process, Trial," *Research Papers in Education* 33, no. 5 (2018): 561–598.

5. See TeachingWorks, "High-Leverage Practices," accessed July 2, 2023, https://library.teachingworks.org/curriculum-resources/high-leverage -practices/; Deborah D. Ball and David K. Cohen, "Developing Practice, Developing Practitioners: Toward a Practice-Based Theory of Professional Education," in *Teaching as the Learning Profession: Handbook of Policy and Practice*, ed. Gary Sykes and Linda Darling-Hammond (San Francisco: Jossey Bass, 1999), 3–32.

6. Pam Grossman and Morva McDonald, "Back to the Future: Directions for Research in Teaching and Teacher Education," *American Educational Research Journal* 45, no. 1 (2008): 184–205.

7. John Dewey, "The Relation of Theory to Practice in Education," in *The Third Yearbook*, ed. NSSSE (Chicago: Bloomington, 1904), 9–39; Grossman and McDonald, "Back to the Future," 189.

8. Morva McDonald, Elham Kazemi, and Sarah Schneider Kavanagh, "Core Practices and Pedagogies of Teacher Education: A Call for a Common Language and Collective Activity," *Journal of Teacher Education* 64, no. 5 (2013): 378–386. See also Pam Grossman, ed., *Teaching Core Practices in Teacher Education* (Cambridge, MA: Harvard Education Press, 2018).

9. Alexander Gröschner et al., "How Systematic Video Reflection in Teacher Professional Development Regarding Classroom Discourse Contributes to Teacher and Student Self-Efficacy," *International Journal of Educational Research* 90 (2018): 223–233; Sarah Michaels, Cathy O'Connor, and Lauren B. Resnick, "Deliberative Discourse Idealized and Realized: Accountable Talk in the Classroom and in Civic Life," *Studies in Philosophy and Education* 27, no. 4 (2008): 283–297.

10. Dewey, "Relation of Theory to Practice," 17.

11. Pam Grossman et al., "Teaching Practice: A Cross-Professional Perspective," *Teachers College Record* 111, no. 9 (2009): 2055–2100.

12. Nicholas C. Burbules, *Dialogue in Teaching: Theory and Practice* (New York: Teachers College Press, 1993).

13. Lauren B. Resnick, Christa Asterhan, and Sherice N. Clarke, eds., *Socializing Intelligence Through Academic Talk and Dialogue* (Washington, DC: AERA, 2015); Rupert Higham, Sue Brindley, and Janneke van de Pol, "Shifting the Primary Focus: Assessing the Case for Dialogic Education in Secondary Classrooms," *Language and Education* 28, no. 1 (2014): 86–99; Luisa Mameli and Consuelo Molinari, "Teaching Interactive Practices and Burnout: A Study on Italian Teachers," *European Journal of Psychology of Education* 32, no. 2 (2017): 219–234; Ian Wilkinson et al., "Toward a More Dialogic Pedagogy: Changing Teachers' Beliefs and Practices Through Professional Development in Language Arts Classrooms," *Language and Education* 31, no. 1 (2017):

65–82; Alexander Gröschner et al., "Through the Lens of Teacher Professional Development Components: The 'Dialogic Video Cycle' as an Innovative Program to Foster Classroom Dialogue," *Professional Development in Education* 41, no. 4 (2015): 729–756.

14. Magdalene Lampert, "Learning Teaching in, from, and for Practice: What Do We Mean?," *Journal of Teacher Education* 61, no. 1–2 (2010): 21–34.

15. Hilda Borko et al., "Video as a Tool for Fostering Productive Discussions in Mathematics Professional Development," *Teaching and Teacher Education* 24, no. 2 (2008): 417–436.

16. Martina Alles, Tina Seidel, and Alexander Gröschner, "Establishing a Positive Learning Atmosphere and Conversation Culture in the Context of a Video-Based Teacher Learning Community," *Professional Development in Education* 45, no. 2 (2019): 250–263; Alexander Gröschner et al., "Facilitating Collaborative Teacher Learning: The Role of 'Mindfulness' in Video-Based Teacher Professional Development Programs," *Gruppendynamik und Organisationsberatung* 45, no. 3 (2014): 273–290.

17. See Dennis Hauk et al., "How Is the Design of Teacher Professional Development Related to Teacher Learning About Classroom Discourse? Findings from a One-Year Intervention Study," *Journal of Education for Teaching* (2022), https://doi.org/10.1080/02607476.2022.2152315; Ann-Kathrin Schindler et al., "Acknowledging Teachers' Individual Starting Conditions and Zones of Development in the Course of Professional Development," *Teaching and Teacher Education* 100 (2021), https://doi.org/10.1016/j.tate.2021.103281.

18. Howe and Abedin, "Classroom Dialogue," 325–356; Mercer, Wegerif, and Major, *Routledge International Handbook of Research on Dialogic Education*; Gaowei Chen and Carol K. K. Chan, "Visualization- and Analytics-Supported Video-Based Professional Development for Promoting Mathematics Classroom Discourse," *Learning, Culture and Social Interaction* 33 (2022):100609, https://doi.org/10.1016/j.lcsi.2022.100609.

19. See Elizabeth A. van Es and Miriam G. Sherin, "Expanding on Prior Conceptualizations of Teacher Noticing," *ZDM—Mathematics Education* 53 (2021): 17–27; Marc Kleinknecht and Alexander Gröschner, "Fostering Pre-service Teachers' Noticing with Structured Video-Feedback: Results of an Online- and Video-Based Intervention Study," *Teaching and Teacher Education* 59 (2016): 45–56; Niels Brouwer, *Using Video to Develop Teaching* (London: Routledge, 2022).

20. Kai S. Cortina and Mark H. Thames, "Teacher Education in Germany," in *Cognitive Activation in the Mathematics Classroom and Professional Competence of Teachers*, Mathematics Teacher Education 8, ed. Mareike Kunter et al. (Boston: Springer, 2013), 49–62.

21. McDonald, Kazemi, and Schneider Kavanagh, "Core Practices and Pedagogies," 378–386; Grossman et al., "Teaching Practice," 2055–2100.

22. Dewey, "Relation of Theory to Practice," 9–39.

23. Hans Gerhard Klinzing, "How Effective Is Micro-teaching? A Survey of Fifty-Three Years of Research," *Zeitschrift für Pädagogik* 48, no. 2 (2002): 194–214.

24. Glenda Anthony, Jodie Hunter, and Roberta Hunter, "Supporting Prospective Teachers to Notice Students' Mathematical Thinking Through Rehearsal Activities," *Mathematics Teacher Education and Development* 17, no. 2 (2015): 7–24; Sarah Schneider Kavanagh et al., "Practicing Responsiveness: Using Approximations of Teaching to Develop Teachers' Responsiveness to Students' Ideas," *Journal of Teacher Education* 71, no. 1 (2020): 94–107; Kiomi Matsumoto-Royo and María Soledad Ramírez-Montoya, "Core Practices in Practice-Based Teacher Education: A Systematic Literature Review of its Teaching and Assessment Process," *Studies in Educational Evaluation* 70 (September 2021): 101047, https://doi.org/10.1016/j.stueduc.2021.101047.

25. Kleinknecht and Gröschner, "Fostering Pre-service Teachers' Noticing," 45–56; Alexander Gröschner et al., "Knowledge Acquisition About Classroom Discourse During a Teaching Practicum? Main and Differential Effects from an Experimental Study" (manuscript in preparation).

CHAPTER 7

1. Reidar Mosvold, Janne Fauskanger, and Kjersti Wæge, "Fra Undervisningskunnskap i Matematikk til Kjernepraksiser—Endringer i Grunnskolelærerutdanningens Matematikkfag," *Uniped: Tidsskrift for universitets—og høgskolepedagogikk* 41, no. 4 (2018): 187–197.

2. Pam Grossman, Sarah Schneider Kavanagh, and Christopher G. Pupik Dean, "The Turn Towards Practice in Teacher Education," in *Teaching Core Practices in Teacher Education*, ed. Pam Grossman (Cambridge, MA: Harvard Education Press, 2018).

3. Advisory Panel for Teacher Education (APT), *Transforming Norwegian Teacher Education: The Final Report of the International Advisory Panel for Primary and Lower Secondary Teacher Education* (Oslo: NOKUT, 2020): 47–48.

4. For example, Hala Ghousseini, "Rehearsals of Teaching and Opportunities to Learn Mathematical Knowledge for Teaching," *Cognition and Instruction* 35, no. 3 (2017): 188–211, https://doi.org/10.1080/07370008.2017.1323903; Elham Kazemi et al., "Getting Inside Rehearsals: Insights from Teacher Educators to Support Work on Complex Practice," *Journal of Teacher Education* 67, no. 1 (2016): 18–31, https://doi.org/10.1177/0022487115615191;

Magdalena Lampert et al., "Keeping It Complex: Using Rehearsals to Support Novice Teacher Learning of Ambitious Teaching," *Journal of Teacher Education* 64, no. 3 (2013): 226–243, https://doi.org/10.1177/0022487112473837.

5. For example, Lynsey K. Gibbons et al., "Teacher Time Out: Educators Learning Together in and Through Practice," *NCSM Journal of Mathematics Education Leadership* 18, no. 2 (2017): 28–45, https://tedd.org/wp-content/uploads/2017/05/JMEL-2017-Teacher-Time-Out.pdf; Kazemi et al., "Getting Inside Rehearsals."

6. Kjersti Wæge and Janne Fauskanger, "Teacher Time Outs in Rehearsals: In-Service Teachers Learning Ambitious Mathematics Teaching Practices," *Journal of Mathematics Teacher Education* 24 (2021): 563–586, https://doi.org/10.1007/s10857-020-09474-0; Kjersti Wæge and Janne Fauskanger, "Supporting In-Service Teachers' Collective Learning of Ambitious Teaching Practices Through Teacher Time Outs," *Scandinavian Journal of Educational Research* 67, no. 4 (2023): 505–520, https://doi.org/10.1080/00313831.2022.2042730.

7. Hala Ghousseini, Heather Beasley, and Sarah Lord, "Investigating the Potential of Guided Practice with an Enactment Tool for Supporting Adaptive Performance," *Journal of the Learning Sciences* 24, no. 3 (2015): 461–497, https://doi.org/10.1080/10508406.2015.1057339; Elham Kazemi, "Teaching a Mathematics Methods Course: Understanding Learning from a Situative Perspective," in *Building Support for Scholarly Practice in Mathematics Methods*, ed. Signe E. Kastberg et al. (Charlotte, NC: Information Age, 2017); Lampert et al., "Keeping It Complex"; Wæge and Fauskanger, "Teacher Time Outs in Rehearsals"; Wæge and Fauskanger, "Supporting In-Service Teachers' Collective Learning."

8. Lampert et al., "Keeping It Complex," 232.

9. For a description of the analysis, see Reidar Mosvold and Kjersti Wæge, "Entailments of Questions and Questioning Practices in Ambitious Mathematics Teaching," *Proceedings of the 12th Congress of European Research in Mathematics Education* (ERME, in press).

10. Meredith D. Gall, "The Use of Questions in Teaching," *Review of Educational Research* 40, no. 5 (1970).

11. Kjersti Wæge and Reidar Mosvold, "Unpacking the Practice of Anticipating Students' Mathematical Responses in Ambitious Mathematics Teaching" (unpublished manuscript, October 27, 2022), Microsoft Word File.

12. Reidar Mosvold and Kjersti Wæge, "Entailments of questions and questioning practices in ambitious mathematics teaching" (paper presented at the 12th Congress of the European Society for Research in Mathematics Education CERME12, Bozen, Italy, February 2022).

13. Anna Sfard and Anna Prusak, "Telling Identities: In Search of an Analytic Tool for Investigating Learning as a Culturally Shaped Activity," *Educational Researcher* 34, no. 4 (2005): 14–22.

14. For a description of the analysis, see Wæge and Fauskanger, "Teacher Time Outs in Rehearsals," 570.

15. Wæge and Fauskanger, "Teacher Time Outs in Rehearsals," 572.

16. Wæge and Fauskanger, "Supporting In-Service Teachers' Collective Learning," 516.

17. Olive Chapman, "Approaches and Challenges in Supporting Mathematics Teachers' Change," *Journal of Mathematics Teacher Education* 19, no. 1 (2016): 1–5, https://doi.org/10.1007/s10857-016-9342-2.

18. Romiett Stevens, *The Question as a Measure of Efficiency in Instruction: A Critical Study of Classroom Practice* (New York: Teachers College, Columbia University, 1912); Hugh Mehan, *Learning Lessons: Social Organization in the Classroom* (Cambridge, MA: Harvard University Press, 1979), 52–65.

19. Allison Hintz and Kersti Tyson, "Complex Listening: Supporting Students to Listen as Mathematical Sense-makers," *Mathematical Thinking and Learning* 17, no. 4 (2015): 292–326, https://doi.org/10.1080/10986065.2015.1084850.

20. Jennifer Richards and Amy D. Robertson, "A Review of the Research on Responsive Teaching in Science and Mathematics," in *Responsive Teaching in Science and Mathematics*, ed. Amy D. Robertson, Rachel Scherr, and David Hammer (New York: Routledge, 2015).

21. Wæge and Fauskanger, "Supporting In-Service Teachers' Collective Learning," 517.

22. Wæge and Fauskanger, "Supporting In-Service Teachers' Collective Learning," 518.

23. Chapman, "Approaches and Challenges in Supporting Mathematics Teachers' Change."

24. Wæge and Fauskanger, "Supporting In-Service Teachers' Collective Learning."

25. See also Wæge and Fauskanger, "Teacher Time Outs in Rehearsals," 579–580.

26. Wæge and Fauskanger, "Supporting In-Service Teachers' Collective Learning," 518.

CHAPTER 8

1. See chapters 3 and 7 in this volume.

2. Pam Grossman, Julia Cohen, and Lindsay Brown, "Understanding Instructional Quality in Language Arts: Variations in the Relationship between PLATO and Value-Added Scores by Content and Context," in *Designing Teacher Evaluation Systems: New Guidance from the Measures of Effective Teaching Project*, ed. Thomas Kane et al. (San Francisco: Jossey-Bass, 2014).

3. Doug Lemov, *Teach Like a Champion: 63 Techniques That Put Students on a Path to College* (San Francisco: Jossey-Bass, 2021); Pam Grossman, Karen Hammerness, and Morva McDonald, "Redefining Teaching, Re-imagining Teacher Education," *Teachers and Teaching: Theory and Practice* 15, no. 2 (2009): 273–290, https://doi.org/10.1080/13540600902875340.

4. See chapters 2, 3, 5, and 7 in this volume.

5. Pam Grossman and Christopher G. Pupik Dean, "Negotiating a Common Language and Shared Understanding About Core Practices: The Case of Discussion," *Teaching and Teacher Education* 80 (2019): 157–166.

6. Identification of core practices of teaching has relied heavily on research on teaching both within subject matter domains and more general research on teaching. Similarly, this work has been informed by theoretical work in the social sciences, particularly by sociocultural theories of teaching and learning. See, for example, the original framework on the teaching of practice (Pam Grossman et al., "Teaching Practice: A Cross-Professional Perspective," *Teachers College Record* 111, no. 9 (2009): 2055–2100) and its references to the work of cognitive psychologists such as Anders Ericcson on deliberate practice, social and cultural psychologists including Jean Lave on the role of context in learning, and sociologists of the professions including Howard Becker.

7. Bradley Fogo, "Core Practices for Teaching History: The Results of a Delphi Panel Survey," *Theory and Research in Social Education* 42, no. 2 (2014): 151–196; Mark Windschitl, Jessica Thompson, and Melissa Braaten, *Ambitious Science Teaching* (Cambridge MA: Harvard Education Press, 2018).

8. "High-Leverage Practices," TeachingWorks, accessed August 29,2023, https://www.teachingworks.org/high-leverage-practices/.

9. Hans Aebli, *Zwölf Grundformen des Lernens. Eine Allgemeine Didaktik auf psychologischer Grundlage* (Stuttgart: Klett, 1983).

10. See chapter 2 in this volume.

11. See chapter 7 in this volume.

12. Thomas H. Levine et al., "Exploring the Nature, Facilitators, and Challenges of Program Coherence in a Case of Teacher Education Program Redesign Using Core Practices," *Journal of Teacher Education* 74, no. 1 (2022): 69–84.

13. Grossman et al., "Teaching Practice"; Morva McDonald, Elham Kazemi, and Sarah Schneider Kavanagh, "Core Practices and Pedagogies of Teacher Education: A Call for a Common Language and Collective Activity," *Journal of Teacher Education* 64, no. 5 (2013): 378–386.

14. See chapter 7 in this volume.

15. See chapter 6 in this volume.

16. See chapter 5 in this volume.

17. See chapters 2 and 7 in this volume.

18. See chapter 4 in this volume.

19. Sarah Schneider Kavanagh, "Practice-Based Teacher Education: Surveying the Landscape, Considering Critiques, and Exploring Future Directions" (white paper for the Spencer Foundation, in press); Dana Grosser-Clarkson and Michael Neel, "Contrast, Commonality, and a Call for Clarity: A Review of the Use of Core Practices in Teacher Education," *Journal of Teacher Education* 71, no. 4 (2020): 464–476.

20. Deborah Loewenberg Ball, "With an Eye on the Mathematical Horizon: Dilemmas of Teaching Elementary School Mathematics," *Elementary School Journal* 93, no. 4 (1993): 373–397.

21. Grossman et al., "Teaching Practice"; McDonald, Kazemi, and Kavanagh, "Core Practices and Pedagogies of Teacher Education."

22. See chapter 5 in this volume.

23. See chapter 7 in this volume.

24. Urban Fraefel, *Core Practices of Successful Teachers: Supporting Learning and Managing Instruction* (Lanham: Rowman & Littlefield, 2023).

ACKNOWLEDGMENTS

This book began with an email between the editors about the relationship of Hans Aebli's work on forms of teaching to the more recent work on core and high-leverage practices. From that initial email exchange, we began a conversation about how ideas related to practice-based teacher education have been taken up in different countries at different time periods. Since Aebli's work had not been translated into English, non-German-speaking scholars were unaware of this earlier work, which has so much resonance with the more current research on core practices of teaching. We are grateful that this initial email sparked a productive collaboration and an ongoing conversation.

We also want to acknowledge the scholars who contributed to this book, who have been so gracious in responding not only to the initial invitation but also to multiple rounds of feedback and revision. We have learned so much from all of them and are inspired by the ways in which they have taken up and extended the ideas and frameworks related to teaching core practices in their own national contexts. We look forward to continuing opportunities to collaborate and learn from one another.

We were fortunate to be able to work with Jayne Fargnoli of Harvard Education Press and her team. Having an editor who supports the work from beginning to end is a gift for which we are very grateful. We also want to acknowledge Jennifer Moore, editor extraordinaire of Penn Graduate School of Education, for her work on the manuscript.

We also want to acknowledge the community of scholars and teacher educators who have experimented with and extended the initial ideas related to practice-based teacher education. This book is dedicated to teacher educators across the world for their tireless work in preparing the next generation of teachers.

ABOUT THE EDITORS

PAM GROSSMAN is the dean of the Graduate School of Education and the George and Diane Weiss Professor of Education at the University of Pennsylvania. A distinguished scholar, she came to Penn from Stanford University's School of Education, where she was the Nomellini-Olivier Professor of Education. At Stanford she founded and led the Center to Support Excellence in Teaching and established the Hollyhock Fellowship for early career teachers in underserved schools.

Dr. Grossman's research focuses on the preparation of teachers and other professionals and issues of instructional quality, particularly in English language arts. Her most recent work focuses on practice-based teacher education and the role of core practices of teaching in teacher preparation and professional development. She has served as chair of the board for the Spencer Foundation and also served on the board of the Carnegie Foundation for the Advancement of Teaching. She was elected to the National Academy of Education in 2009 and to the American Academy of Arts and Sciences in 2017. She currently serves as vice president of the National Academy of Education.

URBAN FRAEFEL is professor emeritus of the School of Education at the University of Applied Sciences and Arts of Northwestern Switzerland, where he established and coordinated the structures and research activities of Studies on Professional Practice. In the years before the emeritus, he was also director of the Institute of Secondary Education. Previously, he was in charge of the teaching and learning of science at the secondary level at the University of Zurich. He was then a member of the founding council of the School of Education Zurich, where he was responsible for the development of the department of field experiences and for the division of educational psychology.

In recent years, Professor Fraefel's research focuses on practice-based education of student teachers in collaboration between universities and schools, assessment of competencies in professional practice, and core practices of teaching, especially in initial teacher education. In addition to publications in these fields, he is also a textbook author. He is also the founder and honorary president of the International Society for Studies on Professional Practice and Professionalization (IGSP).

ABOUT THE CONTRIBUTORS

JANETTE BOBIS is a mathematics educator and researcher in the Sydney School of Education and Social Work at The University of Sydney. She teaches in the areas of primary and early childhood mathematics education and curriculum studies at the undergraduate and graduate levels.

GØRIL BRATAAS is a doctoral research fellow in the Department of Teacher Education and School Research at the University of Oslo. Her interests include mentoring, video as an instructional tool, and practice-based teacher education.

ELISA CALCAGNI is a postdoctoral researcher at the Chair of Research on Teaching and Learning, Friedrich Schiller University Jena, Germany (2020–present); she holds a BA in psychology (2011), an MA in educational psychology (2012), and a PhD in education, University of Cambridge (2020). Her research interests include classroom dialogue, teacher learning, teacher inquiry.

SEBASTIAAN DÖNSZELMANN is a teacher educator and researcher at Vrije Universiteit Amsterdam, working with preservice and in-service teachers in secondary education. He specializes in second language acquisition and professional development of teachers and teacher educators. Sebastiaan's research focuses on effective target language use and acquiring new pedagogical skills within the teaching context.

JANNE FAUSKANGER is a professor in mathematics education at the Faculty of Arts and Education, Department of Education and Sports Science, at the University of Stavanger, Norway. From 2016 she has been working as professor II in mathematics education at the Norwegian Centre for Mathematics Education, Norwegian University for Science and Technology. Her main research interests are teachers' mathematical knowledge for teaching, their teaching practices, and how (student) teachers can learn to enact ambitious teaching practices.

ALEXANDER GRÖSCHNER is chair professor of research on teaching and learning, Friedrich Schiller University Jena, Germany (2016–present), where he leads the Learning-to-Teach Lab: Science; he holds an MA in communication studies, education sciences, and political science (2003); a PhD in educational psychology (2008); and Venia Legendi for Empirical Education Research from Technical University of Munich (2014). He is an associate member of the Cambridge Educational Dialogue Research Group (CEDiR). His research interests include classroom dialogue, teaching quality, video-based teacher learning, teacher professional development, and practice-based teacher education.

INGA STAAL JENSET is an associate professor and head of studies at the Department of Teacher Education and School Research (ILS) at the University of Oslo. Her work focuses on practice-based teacher education and pedagogies of teacher education, including the use of classroom protocols for teacher development. She leads one of the thematic areas in the Nordic Centre of Excellence in Education Quality in Nordic Teaching (QUINT), with a special responsibility for developing video-based teacher training.

ANNA KAAL is a teacher educator and researcher at Vrije Universiteit Amsterdam. She works with preservice and in-service teachers of different disciplines in secondary education. She specializes in foreign language education ("language awareness" and teachers' professional development) and (student) teacher reflection on practice. An essential theme in her work is the notion of "language awareness," which can perhaps best be described as "looking at the world through linguistic glasses": Which knowledge about language do we all need in order to think critically about, but also enjoy, the language we use?

SUSI KLAß is a postdoctoral researcher at the Chair of Research on Teaching and Learning, Friedrich Schiller University Jena, Germany (2017—present).

She holds an MA in media studies and education sciences (2011) and a PhD in education, University of Erlangen-Nuremberg (2017). Her research interests include practice-based teacher education, digitalization and technology use in teacher education, and classroom dialogue.

MARC KLEINKNECHT is chair professor of teacher education and school development at the Leuphana University of Lüneburg, Germany. He holds degrees as a teacher (2000) and in education (2005), a PhD in educational science (2010), and Venia Legendi for Educational Science from Technical University of Munich (2016). His research interests include teaching quality, video-based teacher learning, and practice-based teacher education. In current studies, he is investigating the impact of classroom-video-based feedback of peers and experts on teachers' professional vision and teaching practices.

KIRSTI KLETTE is a professor of classroom studies and curriculum and instruction at the University of Oslo and the director of the research group Studies of Instruction across Subjects and Competences (SISCO) at the Faculty of Educational Sciences. She leads the Teaching Learning Video Lab Oslo and directs the Nordic Centre of Excellence in Education Quality in Nordic Teaching (QUINT), with a special responsibility for video documentation / comparative classroom studies. Her areas of research are teaching and learning in classrooms, video documentation of classroom learning, measurement of instructional quality, and teacher education.

REIDAR MOSVOLD is a professor in mathematics education at the Department of Education and Sports Science at the University of Stavanger, Norway, and he is professor II at the Norwegian Centre for Mathematics Education. His main research interests revolve around research on mathematics teaching, with particular emphasis on what it means to be "smart" in mathematics, the work of leading mathematical discussions, and methods for studying mathematics teaching.

MATTHIAS NÜCKLES is an educational psychologist and full professor of educational science at the University of Freiburg, Germany. In his research, he investigates how students' self-regulated learning can be effectively supported and how teacher education should be designed to promote the acquisition of core practices in teaching. In his interdisciplinary research, Matthias Nückles aims to integrate ideas from educational, social, and cognitive psychology, as well as from the philosophy of science. Furthermore, he teaches lectures and courses on current issues in educational psychology and instructional design.

KURT REUSSER is professor emeritus of education and educational psychology at University of Zürich. After an early career as school teacher and teacher educator, he was trained as an educational psychologist and cognitive scientist in Bern and Boulder, Colorado. His research agenda and his list of publications encompass the broad field of learning and instruction, including general didactics, large scale (inter)national video studies on classroom teaching in mathematics (TIMSS) and history, learner-centered instruction, and teacher education.

KJERSTI WÆGE is the director of the Norwegian Centre for Mathematics Education, which is hosted by the Norwegian University of Science and Technology. Her main research interests include the topics of student motivation, ambitious mathematics teaching, and the relationship between theory and practice in teacher training and professional development.

HANNA WESTBROEK is a researcher and teacher educator at the Vrije University Amsterdam. She teaches courses in chemistry education and action research. She is specifically interested in implications of an ecological perspective on teaching: how work contexts and the way we make decisions in such contexts influence teacher agency and teacher learning. Recent projects concern theory use by school-based mentors and how school-based mentors can use the goal system methodology in their mentoring practices (with Anna Kaal). She co-supervises PhD and postdoctoral projects on teacher agency and on enhancing chemical and biological thinking in the classroom.

INDEX